Lutheran

*none*

# RELIGIOUS

OR

# CHRISTIAN

BY

O. HALLESBY, Ph.D.

*Professor in the Independent Theological Seminary*
*Oslo, Norway*

TRANSLATED BY

CLARENCE J. CARLSEN

2478
HAL

Christianity
Christian Living
Doctrine
Faith

1959
198

*Lutheran*

PUBLISHED BY

AUGSBURG PUBLISHING HOUSE

MINNEAPOLIS, MINNESOTA

*Eleventh Printing,* 1959

Printed by Augsburg Publishing House, Minneapolis 15, Minnesota
Manufactured in the United States of America
. . . 3750 . . .

# Preface

THE great danger threatening Christianity throughout the ages has not been opposition and persecution, but that of blending and confounding Christianity with pagan religion.

It was a mixture of this kind that *Gnosticism* sought to compound.

And it was as a result of a syncretism of this kind that the great *Nestorian* church in India and China succumbed to Buddhism in the Middle Ages, leaving scarcely a trace of itself.

Toward the close of antiquity Christianity in *North Africa* was compelled to give way to Mohammedanism for the same reason.

Also *Roman Catholicism,* presenting as it has from the beginning of the Middle Ages and down to our day a world-wide, unevangelical, yea, anti-evangelical type of religiosity, recognized by both culture and politics, is a fruit of the most grandiose mixing of religions known to history.

In more recent times, from the age of the *Renaissance* and down through the period of *Socinianism* and *rationalism,* a new syncretism of religion on a grand scale has been and still is in process in Protestant lands. It threatens to completely eradicate Christianity from Europe and to introduce in its stead a rationalistic-gnostic religion fashioned out of elements taken from the religions of all the ages and from every corner of the earth.

These brief devotional articles are sent forth as a modest attempt to ward off this danger. They are not intended as a *theoretical* reckoning between heathenism and Christianity, but as an unpretentious attempt in a practical way to afford guidance to those who at this time, in our subtly dangerous age of syncretism, would know the difference between religion and Christianity, that their souls might be saved.

O. HALLESBY.

# Contents

# Christianity's Intellectual Crosses

ALL religion contains an element which is a cross to the intellect, because religion deals with the *absolute*. It is the paradoxical element. The intellectual crosses arise at the point where the absolute and the relative meet.

The less a religion brings us face to face with the absolute, the fewer intellectual crosses it will have. For that reason Christianity has more intellectual crosses than any other religion.

Now, the intellectual crosses of Christianity occur on various planes.

As intellectual crosses they all have a rational aspect. But that which causes our intellectual difficulties may occur in various realms of the spirit of man, in the realm of the *intellectual*, of the *moral*, or of the *religious*.

Let us consider first the intellectual crosses.

Modern man no doubt feels that he encounters an intellectual cross in Christianity at nearly every step of the way. Let us begin with the doctrine of God.

God is triune. By this we do not mean three different forms of revelation of the one God. Not at all; these three are eternal *I am's* or persons. And still Christianity teaches that there are not three gods, but one God.

Christ is God and man. And, be it noted well, not alternatingly; not first God, then man, and then God again. That, too, would constitute a difficulty, undoubtedly. But the difficulty becomes even greater when Chris-

tianity says that Christ is God and man at one and the
same time.

Christianity says further that He was conceived by the
Holy Spirit and born of a virgin.

He performed a multitude of acts which seem to be in
conflict with reality as we know it. For instance, He
healed the sick or the mentally diseased *by a word*. He
raised the dead. He walked upon water. He fed thou-
sands with five loaves and two fishes.

He was unlike the rest of us, not only in life, but also
in *death*. His suffering and death were an atonement, a
substitutionary atonement, for the sins of all men.

Moreover, death could not hold Him. He arose bodily
from the grave on the third day. Not as Lazarus of
Bethany, who had to die again. Jesus arose unto an in-
corruptible life, over which death has no power.

A short time later He ascended into heaven. But before
He did so, He instituted two remarkable ordinances,
*Baptism* and the *Lord's Supper,* which are different from
all other ordinances of which we have any knowledge. As
the church pours water upon the child, Christ performs
invisibly an inner act known as *regeneration*. And as we
partake of the bread and the wine, Christ imparts to us
His *body* and His *blood*.

Finally, we might mention *prayer* and *answers to
prayer*. Christ has promised, not only to hear, but also to
fulfill, the petitions of His friends; and thus effect changes
in the divine government of the universe, simply because
a human being asks Him to do so.

Summarizing we may say:

The intellectual paradoxes of Christianity converge
upon the *miracle* as their focal point. In the miracle it is
the *supernatural* which constitutes the intellectual cross,
not only because modern science with practical unanimity
*denies* miracles, but in particular because modern science

*excludes* the very possibility of miracles, by the method which it employs. The miracle conflicts with the very idea of reality which is held by modern science.

This comes to light in a typical manner in historical research. By its very method it lays down the postulate that a historical source which contains accounts of miracles must, for this reason alone, be classified as a secondary source, regardless of what judgment one might otherwise pass regarding its historical value.

Let us turn to intellectual crosses in the *moral* realm. Here we must mention in the first place the *origin* of sin, the fact that the whole race is sinful because the first man fell into sin.

In the next place, the *propagation* of sin, the fact that both sin and guilt are inherited.

Further, the *punishment* of sin. A great deal could be said about this. I shall mention, however, only the greatest intellectual cross in this connection, the fact that God has decreed *eternal* suffering as punishment for sin.

Finally, the *nature* of sin, namely, that man is *evil,* and cannot therefore either individually or collectively be made inherently *better,* but can only be *saved,* and that by being *created anew* completely.

Let us consider briefly the intellectual crosses in the realm of the *religious.*

The chief intellectual cross we encounter here is the Bible's unique *concept* of holiness, the most offensive expression of which is the doctrine of the *wrath* of God. This concept is so fundamental to both the Old Testament and the New that salvation is in reality salvation from the wrath of God.

The average modern man feels that it is more like profanation than anything else to speak of the wrath of God, about as blasphemous as to speak of sin in God.

The *grace* of God is no less an intellectual cross.

The difficulty does not consist in the fact that God forgives one who has sinned against Him, but in the fact that He first requires atonement, which His own eternal Son takes upon Himself to make, and which consists in this, that the Son vicariously suffers the wrath and punishment of God which hitherto has rested upon man.

Then we have the salvation of the individual, that which the Scriptures speak of as *justification.* It consists in this, that God justifies the *ungodly,* simply because he believes in Jesus Christ.

What Scripture means by *regeneration* is no less offensive.

Regeneration emphasizes more strongly than anything else Christianity's *pessimistic* view of man. No one can enter into Christian fellowship with God by his own moral efforts, only by a divine new-creation.

To the average person this seems to weaken man's sense of responsibility. Instead of appealing to man's will, Christians give themselves up to a mysterious experience of God, and thus seem to weaken the moral requirement.

In summing up this matter of intellectual crosses in the realm of the religious, we might say that Christianity endows God with attributes which seem to be definitely at variance with an ethical concept of God.

+

Toward these various intellectual crosses in Christianity somewhat different attitudes are taken by different people.

By way of survey permit me to mention three of the various positions that are taken, not only because they are the most *common* in our day, but also because they are the most typical.

First, I would mention those who *reject Christianity* entirely because of these intellectual difficulties.

They do not say so as politely as the aged Bjørnson did when he, in bidding adieu to Christianity, voiced the opinion that it was beyond him. On the contrary, they say that Christianity is beneath criticism, that not only intellectually, but also morally and religiously, it is on such a low plane that no modern person, who is somewhat informed and intelligent, can take cognizance of it.

In the second place, I would mention those who think that it is not at all necessary to reject Christianity, even though one must reject the intellectual crosses that we have mentioned.

Those adhering to this viewpoint are of the opinion that these crosses have essentially nothing to do with Christianity. These intellectual crosses are not an expression of Christianity in its original and true form, but are, rather, immature expressions of the attempts of previous ages to *think* Christianity.

These thought-forms, which were natural and which served the purpose of past generations, are now antiquated. As a result of the tremendous progress that has taken place both in the mental and in the natural sciences, this intellectual garb of Christianity is not only unmodern, but impractical, and a hindrance to Christianity.

Our problem is therefore to relieve Christianity of its antiquated intellectual garb and free it from those intellectual crosses which more than anything else hinder modern men from opening their hearts and minds to the eternal and unchangeable religious truths of Christianity.

And with the whole scientific apparatus which is at the disposal of our age they undertake the tremendous task of differentiating between the *shell* and the *kernel* of Christianity, of cutting through all the pious and well-meant theology of the church, all mythology and legend, and arriving at the *gospel of Jesus,* or rather, the *religion of Jesus,* from the paradoxical Christ of faith to the simple Jesus of history.

Regardless of what some may think of these efforts, it must be conceded that they have in truth succeeded in presenting a religion which is comparatively free from intellectual crosses.

If it is a religion without paradoxes that modern man is seeking, he has indeed reached the goal of his desires!

+

But there is one aspect of this question of which we are compelled to be somewhat critical, namely, that this religion without paradoxes is represented as Christianity, as a matter of fact, as real, original Christianity.

One is even more surprised to note that this is done in the name of *science,* even in the name of the *science of comparative* religion.

Many seem to be so enthusiastic over what science has accomplished in this connection that they have not as yet discovered the unheard of *crime* which has been committed in the name of science—the crime of striking out in the name of religious research all historical Christianity, all of Christianity's nineteen centuries of history. No greater sin—none with such ramifications—has ever been committed against the science of comparative religion.

In the name of this science men quietly close their eyes to the fact that during all these 1900 years Christianity has contained all the intellectual crosses that we have mentioned above, in fact, that this religion through all these centuries has taught that these mental crosses, this paradoxical and irrational faith-content, are synonymous with that living reality which is Christianity.

In the name of the history of religion they have perpetrated the religio-historical *monstrosity* of *not* conducting research into what the Christian religion historically and factually has been and still is. On the contrary, they apply all of their religio-scientific strength and ability to the task of showing what Christianity *should have been* and what it therefore *should be* today.

Try to imagine a specialist in the history of religion doing the same thing to some other religion, Buddhism or Mohammedanism, for instance. Imagine him paying no attention to its historical nature, its religious peculiarity, and instead trying to show what it *ought* to have been.

It is, of course, unthinkable that any scholar would do this with other religions. In those fields they work in accordance with the universally recognized scientific requirement of complete *objectivity, sine ira et studio,* as the ancients expressed it in Latin.

It is only when dealing with Christianity that these scholars become so preoccupied that they overlook the most elementary laws governing scientific research. They are so interested personally in providing a religion without paradoxes for modern man that they seek to *construe* the historical and religious character of Christianity instead of *establishing* it.

But what attitude *should* we take toward these paradoxes of the Christian faith?

If we cannot, in accordance with the first mentioned viewpoint, give up Christianity entirely because of its intellectual crosses, and if we cannot accept the last named viewpoint and construe history thus, which is essentially the same as to falsify history, to falisfy the whole history of Christianity, what then shall we do?

There is scarcely any prospect that we shall all find ourselves in agreement when attempting to give an answer to *this* question.

But perhaps we could come to partial agreement.

In the first instance, we might agree that the attitude of

all of us toward Christianity and its intellectual crosses rests upon a *choice*.

Secondly, that this choice is not made upon a scientific plane, upon scientific premises or considerations. Whether I accept or reject Christianity, it is not science that determines my choice.

Not longer than twenty years ago a modern man would have protested against a statement of this kind. Today, however, modern man knows more than he formerly did also about the relationship between science and religion. The talk about accepting or rejecting Christianity upon scientific grounds, which formerly was so common, is now considered equally as absurd as talking about seeing with one's ears or hearing with one's nose.

Choice of religion takes place from religious or moral motives. The same is true of the attitude that each of us takes toward the intellectual crosses connected with Christianity.

In speaking briefly about this choice, I desire first to say a few words about the *history of such choices.*

Here I would begin again by pointing out the simple but very important fact that there has never existed any such thing as Christianity without the intellectual crosses which I have mentioned.

I am of course aware of the fact that at various times in the history of the church there have been certain individuals who have protested against a greater or lesser number of these intellectual crosses. But nevertheless it is an incontrovertible historical fact that all the Christian churches throughout all these centuries have not only confessed, but have also been fully conscious of what they were doing when they emphasized that these intellectual crosses were the very heart of the Christian faith.

We have the most elementary proof of this in the so-called *ecumenical* confessions, that is, the confessions that are common to all Christian churches, namely, the Apostolic, the Nicene, and the Athanasian creeds.

In these the Christian church has gathered up in very brief summary the whole content of its faith. And here we find, as a matter of fact, all the intellectual crosses that we have mentioned.

Moreover, research has shown that one of these confessions, the Apostolic, dates all the way back to the apostolic age, even though in the very earliest period it did not have exactly the same form as we use now.

We can thus trace the history of these intellectual crosses all the way back to the time in which Christianity originated and to its classical documents, the New Testament writings. We discover, moreover, that in these very writings we have the source of the whole paradoxical, irrational content of the faith which the Christian church has owned, confessed, and preached throughout all these centuries.

This simple historical fact solves a very important problem in connection with these intellectual crosses. It does not solve the intellectual problems themselves, but it does make clear their relationship to Christianity. It tells us with factual authority that these intellectual crosses are an organic, indispensable part of genuine, historical Christianity.

+

Now, we know that many people think that modern man is the first to have experienced these crosses. They think that men in ancient times did not feel them as such.

However, this idea is not based upon any real study of the sources; it is an arbitrary assumption. The epistles and the Book of Acts in the New Testament tell us something very different about ancient man, namely, that apostolic preaching was a *stumbling-block* to the Jews and

*foolishness* to the Greeks. This the apostle Paul, for example, experienced in full measure.

The gospels tell us the same story.

Most of the Jews were more or less interested in Jesus
of Nazareth, perhaps with the exception of the *cultured
Jews* of that day, the Sadducees. The latter did not seem
to take any notice of Jesus, at least not until they began to
fear His following from a political standpoint.

The *scholarly* authorities of that day, the scribes, and
the *churchly* authorities, the Pharisees, took a greater and
more friendly interest in Him. But though they made
approaches to Him, nevertheless they rejected Him.

In this one respect they were in agreement with their
opponents, the Sadducees.

What was there about Christ that caused them to reject
Him?

It was the paradoxes. It was the paradox of paradoxes
that He said of Himself that He was God (John 10:33).

Modern man always takes offense at these intellectual
crosses.

And modern man has been in existence throughout the
ages. You young people are modern today. In twenty-five
years you will be left behind by those who will then be
young, who will then be the moderns. Nineteen hundred
years ago the Sadducees, the Pharisees, and the scribes
were the moderns of their day. And they took offense at
the paradoxical element in the person of Jesus. We read
in the gospels how they criticized Him and sought to
enlighten Him as to what the Messiah should be and how
He should conduct Himself. As a matter of fact, they made
the direct proposal that if He would agree with them they
would provide Him with that following among the people
which He sought.

Jesus Himself was fully aware of the offending intellectual cross which He was both in His person and in His

work. But He never minimized this cross in order to gain followers. We recall His sad words when He saw what effect this intellectual cross had upon the people of that day: "Blessed is he, whosoever shall find no occassion of stumbling in me" (Matthew 11 :6).

The New Testament and the history of Christianity make it clear to us, then, that there is an intellectual cross which cannot be separated from the person and work of Christ. I cannot dissociate the intellectual cross from Christ. Either I must choose Christ *and the intellectual cross,* or reject the intellectual cross *and Christ.*

*

But as soon as *this* becomes clear to me, that to be a Christian has at all times been identical with believing in the paradoxical Christ, then the question arises : how did it come about? How *could* people believe thus? How could they believe in such a Christ without being untrue to themselves? without committing a "sacrificium intellectus," deliberate intellectual suicide?

Now, I note from Christian history, in the first place, the remarkable fact that Christian people themselves have not felt that faith in the paradoxical Christ was offensive to their intellect.

If these people had been only such as were unaccustomed to scholarly and exact thinking, this fact would not have meant a great deal. But a large number of these Christians down through the centuries have been thinkers of great distinction. Permit me only to mention such men as Paul, Augustine, Luther, Calvin, Pascal, and Kierkegaard.

This fact tells me that this matter of intellectual crosses is one of those difficult things that is resolved *in life* and not by our *thinking.* There are, as we know, several such phases in that rich and complex life which we know as human life. We generally classify these under the rubric of the *irrational,* that which lies *beyond reason.*

Yes, the intellectual difficulties connected with the paradoxes of the Christian faith are solved *in life.*

That is the very point of the matter. Becoming a Christian never takes place as a result of thinking, even though in adults it never takes place *without* thinking.

It is an *experience* that makes us Christians.

We experience God. It is in Christ that we meet God. And this meeting with God has the same effect upon all of us, regardless of age, sex, class or station in life.

We experience our separation from God, especially our moral separation. We experience that which the Bible speaks of as sin and guilt. Note this well: we *experience* these things.

No doubt we *think* about them also. But that which takes place within us is not fundamentally an affair of the mind. Least of all the things which occur at the turbulent time of one's spiritual awakening. Think of the many seekers after God who are unable to understand themselves. Their ability to think is at a standstill. But their ability to experience things is functioning perfectly. They have met the living God, and holy anxiety has begun to make its way into their frivolous hearts.

No doubt the congenital rationalists within their bosoms institute proceedings against the Lord and seek to interpose all possible mitigating circumstances. But their experience of the divine finally sweeps all this aside like so much cobweb. With flaming letters the truth is burned into their consciences: you do not love God. Not only do you *do* that which is sinful, but you *love* it. Can you with a will thus divided and with your half-heartedness believe that God can have anything to do with you?

It was thus they experienced it, Peter, Paul, Augustine.

Luther, Calvin, Francke, Grundtvig, and Hans Nielsen Hauge.        +

If one has thus met God and had a genuine experience of sin, then there is, so nineteen centuries of Christian history teach us, in all the world no other consolation and help remaining to a sinner but the paradoxical gospel of the paradoxical Saviour, who was God and became man, and suffered and died as an atonement for our sins.

Now, note well that Christianity is fully cognizant of the fact that there are other palliatives for the distress caused by sin, both in Judaism and in paganism.

If one has experienced no other sense of sin and no other distress because of sin than that which Judaism and heathenism produce in man, then one can also find help in the comfort with which *unbelieving* Jews and pagans comfort themselves.

Then you do not need Christ.

Such people are both moral and religious, but they have no use for Christ in their relationship to God. The cross and redemption are superfluous adjuncts to religion as far as they are concerned, and only bring disturbance into their religious circles.

Thus it was with the Sadducees and thus it was with the Pharisees. They were religious people, but there was no room for Christ, the cross, and redemption in their religious system.

Thus it has been through all these 1900 years with all religious people who have not permitted themselves to become completely undone by having a meeting with the living God.

If they are people of the uncritical type, they calmly set aside Christ and the cross and live their paradox-less religion with something they call "God the Father," more or less religiously, more or less rationally, all according to their disposition or their environment.

If they are more reflective and critical by nature, then they proceed to set things aright in the overly complicated field of religion, not concealing in any way their idea that our Lord has taken this matter of our sins altogether too seriously. This whole affair about becoming man to atone for our sins is to them quite superfluous. It is not necessary for God to do anything else but forgive the penitent sinner, who, impelled by religious inclinations and sincere repentance, turns unto God.

+

Entirely different is the case of the sinner who has become completely undone as a result of having met Christ. Think of Peter as he lay at Jesus' feet in the boat, or of Paul as he lay there in the light of the heavenly vision on the road to Damascus. We can be certain that they at that time felt no desire to criticize Christ or remove the paradoxical element in connection with Him. They had become sinners before God; their mouth had been stopped, as Paul on a subsequent occasion expresses it.

Through this experience these men found that their intellectual crosses had been transferred to a different realm.

No longer do *theoretical* questions, about the conception, the atoning death, or the bodily resurrection, cause them difficulty. On the contrary, the intellectual cross which now disturbs them has become a practical one: Is it possible for God to receive a sinner such as I? How can I find a gracious God?

How then can *this* paradox be overcome?

This one cannot be solved by *thinking* either, but by *experience*. By a new experience of *God*.

The sincere soul, who in his meeting with Christ has become completely undone, cannot cope with the sinfulness which has thus been revealed to him, not even by the most desperate moral and religious efforts. However, he cannot refrain from seeking the very God he now feels must turn him away.

During this time his religious life vacillates strongly, between hope and fear, joy and anxiety, peace and despair. Usually he is at a loss as to what to do; seldom is he happy.

Until something again takes place in his life.

Something unthought of, unsuspected, and which he himself has done nothing to bring about. It is God again who takes the initiative, and meets him in an entirely different way. Through the *Word* of the Scriptures.

Outwardly this experience may vary somewhat. But as a rule it takes place when a passage of the Bible opens itself to his soul in a manner hitherto wholly unknown. The passage becomes like a little window, through which he peers into the boundless realm of grace.

That which he then experiences, is not easy to express in words. Let me try to put it this way:

With all the faculties of his soul he absorbs the world's most real reality, the miracle of the grace of God in Christ. The cross, the atonement, forgiveness are experienced with all the clarity and power of *intuition,* in its super-rational connection with the suffering love of the eternal God.

Now doubt and uncertainty are gone. An unspeakable joy and security fill the soul.

This miracle is spoken of in the Scriptures as the experiencing of the Spirit. The Christian church has through the centuries expressed it thus: I believe in the Holy Ghost, . . . the forgiveness of sins.

+

This experience is not founded upon *thinking,* even though it, of course, does not take place apart from thinking.

*Life* reveals itself also here in all its majesty—and puts thinking in its rightful place.

How do the intellectual crosses affect him now?
Does he understand them? Can he think them through?
No, he cannot.
But do they not cause him much mental distress?
No, they do not do that either. Ask Paul, Augustine,
Luther, Pascal, Kierkegaard!
But is this not due to auto-suggestion, to a voluntary
inhibition of the thinking faculty?
Well, let us be critical.
But let us not be so critical that we cannot by personal
observation assure ourselves whether the thinking we find
in the above-mentioned Christian thinkers is cowardly and
superficial or not. I would that all my readers might have
the intellectual joy of reading Paul, Augustine, Luther,
Pascal, Kierkegaard!
Let us on the whole be a little careful about employing
the much misused word auto-suggestion!
There are, as we all know, many paradoxes in life which
cause us no mental difficulty whatsoever. Permit me to
mention some of the most common ones: life, power, time,
space. Not even the most profound scholar *understands*
these realities. Moreover, if he tries to think them through,
he becomes entangled in irreconcilable contradictions.
But do these paradoxes insult the intelligence of modern
man! No, he not only lives his life, but enjoys it to the
fullest extent, even though that life contains intellectual
difficulties which he cannot resolve. Nor does anyone say
anything in this connection about auto-suggestion or the
inhibition of the thinking faculty!
Nay, let no one lead us to imagine that intellectual
crosses are the things that frighten the modern man away
from Christianity.
It is Christianity's *demands* that have frightened and
still do frighten modern man, and will do so to the end
of time. Man refuses to meet God in Christ, for he feels

instinctively that such a meeting will lead to the death of his own *self-centered* life.

You of my readers who are still spectators as far as Christianity is concerned, more or less doubting and wondering spectators, brush aside all your empty phrases and admit to yourselves that it is not the intellectual crosses of Christianity that frighten you, but this, that Christ would make *separation between you and your sins.*

And those of you who would become Christians, regardless of the cost, note this: It is not for you by your own moral and religious exertions to furnish yourselves with an experience of God.

All you are to do is to confess that you do not love God, that you do not even *experience* God, only your own religious thoughts, longings, and efforts!

Then begin to pray that God would have a meeting with you, and provide you with a personal, first-hand, and daily experience of Himself.

Pray for the Holy Spirit, and read your New Testament, every day, with this prayer in your heart.

Then you will become a Christian, that is, you will meet God in Christ.

It will begin as painful mortification.

But thus to be mortified before God is the beginning of life.

# The Obedience of Faith

FAITH-LIFE has many aspects. The Scriptures and experience tell us that obedience is an exceedingly important aspect of faith, but also a very difficult one.

"Behold, to obey is better than sacrifice, and to hearken than the fat of rams" (I Samuel 15:22). When we recall what sacrifice meant according to God's own institution in the Old Covenant, we begin to gain some idea of the value of obedience in the sight of God. The passage we have cited no doubt means that men can bring God no sacrifice, no gift, that is more valuable in His sight than obedience.

But at the same time the Scriptures tell us from cover to cover that no gift is more difficult for us to bring to God than obedience.

Even the most God-fearing men mentioned in the Bible erred by being disobedient. It seems that this was their greatest temptation. Thus, both in the Old Testament and in the New Testament, Moses is pictured as an extraordinary prophet of God (Exodus 33:11; Numbers 12:3, 7, 8; Deuteronomy 34:10-12; Hebrews 3:2). Nevertheless, Moses committed a sin of disobedience so great that the Lord had to mete out to him the severe punishment of not being permitted to enter into the promised land (Numbers 20:7-12). He was excluded as completely as the other disobedient Israelites who had seen the glory of God and the signs He had done in Egypt (Numbers 14:20-23).

In fact, even Christ, God's own Son, had to *learn* obedience (Hebrews 5:8).

And it was through suffering and temptation that He

learned it. His temptation was all along a temptation to disobey the Father's will and not to walk in His way. All three temptations in the wilderness were temptations to disobedience. Likewise the temptation at Caesarea Philippi (Matthew 16:13-23) and at the wedding in Cana (John 2:4).

The gospels do not conceal the fact that obedience was *difficult* even for Jesus. It cost Him terrific struggles. "Who in the days of his flesh, having offered up prayers and supplications with strong crying and tears unto him that was able to save him from death, and having been heard for his godly fear" (Hebrews 5:7). It is prayers and cries of distress such as this that we hear in Gethsemane and upon the cross (Matthew 26:38-44; 27:46).

If I understand the gospels right, obedience was the great test which Jesus was called upon to meet and which determined whether He could become our Saviour. The Scriptures say: "Though he was a Son, yet learned obedience by the things which he suffered; and having been made perfect, he became unto all them that obey him the author of eternal salvation" (Hebrews 5:8-9). And again: "and being found in fashion as a man, he humbled himself, becoming obedient even unto death, yea, the death of the cross. Wherefore God also highly exalted him, and gave unto him the name which is above every name" (Philippians 2:8-9). And: "For as through one man's disobedience the many were made sinners, even so through the *obedience* of one shall the many be made righteous" (Romans 5:19).

Yea, verily, here we have indicated to us the *value* of obedience in the sight of God, as well as its *importance* in connection with our Christian life and our salvation.

✝

## OUR INBRED SPIRIT OF DISOBEDIENCE

The passage cited, Romans 5:19, tells us that our sin was from the very beginning one of disobedience. The sinful mind is the disobedient mind, which does *not desire* to do the will of God, not even when the natural man seeks to do the will of God because he is afraid of God or because he deems it a wise expedient.

The natural man looks upon God as something unpleasant, something annoying, as something that is in his way. He even looks upon God as his adversary or enemy, simply because God is a God who *wills,* a God who wills something very definite in regard to man, a God who wills that which is *right* and true, a God whose will, therefore, is the *strongest* of all wills, in the presence of which man feels, deep in his heart, that he is inferior and impotent.

On one occasion Jesus characterized the flesh as the opposite of *the willing spirit* (Mark 14:38). And the unwilling spirit is precisely the thing which characterizes the natural man. And this is not only true when he leads an *ungodly* or *worldly* life, at which times unregenerate man thinks that God's requirements are so unreasonable that they do not apply to him, wherefore he does as he thinks best himself, or, in doubtful instances, what other people do as a rule.

The natural man's relationship to God is characterized by an unwilling spirit also when he lives a *moral* and *religious* life. In the realm of morals he feels that God's commandments are too numerous and too difficult to observe, wherefore he feels relieved when he can in some way arrange a moral vacation for himself, releasing himself from any obligation to fulfill any of God's moral requirements.

The unwilling spirit manifests itself also in connection with his *religious* association with God. He finds it very strenuous to be religious, that is, to pray to God, to read the Bible every day, to go to church regularly, and, in particular, to be compelled to speak about God and things religious. Except in religious debate; then he can speak fluently, without any unwillingness of spirit or effort. The peculiar thing about this unwilling religious attitude is that it is so temperate, so fearful of exaggeration in religion, that is, of becoming too religious.

Fundamentally, the natural man is both moral and religious. To live without morals or without God is not natural for the natural man. He must force himself to sink down to such a life. The natural man has natural capacities both for morality and religion, but, note well, for "natural" morality and "natural" religion. As strongly opposed as he is to God's morality and God's religion, just so strongly does the religion and the morality which he himself has devised appeal to him.

Therefore we see also that the natural man does not make use of his religion and morality as a means of entering into fellowship with *God* and doing *His* will, but, on the contrary, as a shield against God, and to avoid doing His will. When God, notwithstanding this, unbidden and unwelcome, meets this religious man, we note that it is by means of his religion that such a man is able to fortify himself against God with greatest success and for the longest time.

This comes to light clearly on our mission fields. When the gospel comes to the heathen, it is their religion they make use of as their ultimate means of defense against God's mighty call through the gospel.

We see the same thing here at home.

When God meets a natural man, living a moral and religious life, we notice that this man employs his religion as his best defense against the gospel's urgent requirements of repentance and regeneration. Therefore we see also that none are more bitter and more determined opponents of spiritual awakening and conversion than these selfsame religious people, who have provided themselves with a morality and a religion which they deem sufficient, the very purpose of which is to prevent any further interference on the part of the Lord.

Of course, I do not mean to say that these good and respectable people practice this deception consciously. Not at all; *that,* too, is one of the peculiarities of the natural man, that he feels absolutely safe and above criticism as far as his relation to God is concerned, and considers his own judgment in things pertaining to morality and religion safer and more trustworthy than the divine word of the Scriptures. That is why these people think that they are in the *right* when opposing spiritual awakening and conversion and looking upon such things with disfavor.

Here we are afforded an insight into the depths of the natural man's self-fortified position with respect to God.

Not only does he bear ill will toward God, and not only does he use his religion to shield himself from God's searching eye and mortifying requirements, but he thinks that by so doing he renders God a very great service in connection with "extremeism" in religion, for is he not demonstrating to his fellow men a form of religion which is so temperate that they need not become weary both of God and religion!

It is their profound conviction that it is "extremeism" in Christianity that frightens people away from the Lord. According to their viewpoint, most people would seek the church and our Lord if opportunity were given them to hear and to understand how reasonable the Lord is in His religious requirements. Opposition to God would disappear, and folk would feel that it was easy and pleasant to be religious.

If we have gained an insight into the natural man's inbred opposition to God, his inner revulsion with respect to the will of God, it will be clear to us that the great miracle of salvation consists in this, that God can change disobedient men, such as we are, making them obedient and causing them to choose and to desire to do the will of God voluntarily.

How does He do this?

## THE ORIGIN OF OBEDIENCE

### 1. In Spiritual Awakening

I do not know whether we ever experience anything more mystical and impossible of explanation than our spiritual awakening. Note, for instance, the man who lives an *ungodly* life. He sins so calmly and boldly that he does not even try to conceal his wrong-doing.

Then God comes. And this bold, self-assured sinner begins to experience sin as the most terrible thing in his life. He experiences, too, at the same time, that sin is dearer to him than anything else. As a result he continues to sin. But it is this very unyielding, indomitable *will* to sin which he now feels as his worst, his most terrible, curse.

Or consider the *worldly* person. He is a good, respectable, useful, perhaps also a good-hearted, person. But he has no time and no use for God, at least not for the will of God. Such a person may not be opposed to religious sentiment, a devotional atmosphere, or festive occasions of a religious nature, particularly, and this should be noted well, if there is not too much of it, and above all, if it does not hinder him from living his own self-guided, earth-minded life.

Then God comes. And this world-loving, self-secure man begins to feel as though he is drowning in his own worldliness. He now feels that his worldliness is the curse of his life. And he experiences at the same time that he loves the world and the things of the world, while he both fears and hates the God who disturbs him in his worldliness.

Or note the *religious* man. It may be that he lives an intense, highly emotional, unbalanced religious life. Or his religion may be of a calm, intelligent, and character-emphasizing kind. In either case, religious people of this type feel that they have reached an "agreement" with the Lord, have found a form of religion and morality which has the approval of God. And never does a person become more pleased with himself and more sure of himself than when he has provided himself with a religion by means of which he can "manage" even our Lord Himself.

Then God comes, and disturbs the whole thing. To their utter dismay these people learn that God is not the same as religion. They see now that with all their religion they have not as yet dealt with *God,* only with *themselves.* They discover for the first time that God does not care for their religion, but desires their hearts, their wills. But up to this time these people have never thought of yielding either their hearts or their wills to the Lord.

The natural man feels inherently bitter toward God when He with a heavy hand breaks down his health, deprives him of strength to work, frustrates him in his plans and hopes, or breaks into his family circle and removes his dear ones. But never, in all probability, does the natural man feel more strongly opposed to God than when He with brutal hand also demolishes his religion.

Here we see the *miraculous* aspect of spiritual awakening, its *new-creating* power, the *grace* connected with such an awakening!

In a way that we cannot understand, God has, through the miracle of spiritual awakening, created within the natural man an inescapable feeling of the fact that he is in conflict with the will of God. With painful clarity the

sinner feels that he is doing his own will. At the same
time he feels how terrible it is to do his own will, in
direct violation of the kind and loving will of God.

## 2. In Conversion

Conversion is a choice. However, there are many
choices which are mistaken for the choice involved in
conversion.

In conversion the choice is between my own will and
that of God. This is what produces the anxiety connected
with conversion. We have just spoken of the distress
involved in spiritual awakening, but that associated with
conversion is no less severe. The natural man has, as has
already been shown, an inbred distrust of God and a
natural confidence in himself. This is the reason for his
intense fear of surrendering himself to God, of permitting
the will of God to prevail in his inner as well as in
his outward life. *That* is without doubt the deepest lying
reason why most people avoid, evade, or postpone conversion. To them nothing is so hazardous as to yield
themselves wholly to God. And in order to avoid such
a surrender these people will often make the most unheard
of sacrifices and efforts, religiously speaking, provided
they themselves can sit at the wheel and handle the brakes.

Many think that conversion is a choice whereby I with
all the power of my will declare myself done with my past
life, and with all my heart begin to seek God. It is true
that no true conversion takes places without this. But
this is not really the same as conversion itself.

Conversion is the result of a divine miracle which
causes me to despair of everything that is my own, especially my own will. It has been opposed to the will of
God all along. My unconverted life consisted in this, that
*I* willed, incessantly willed something, namely, that God
be hindered from having His way with me. The choice

involved in conversion consists therefore not in willing to *do* something, but rather in willingness to let something *be done* with me, namely, that God be given access to my life with His will, that will against which I hitherto have sought to barricade myself with all my strength.

To be converted is therefore nothing else but to permit the voice of God to be heard, that voice which I hitherto have permitted to go unheeded, or even have sought to render inaudible by means of my own religion. Now, I will, I choose, that *God* shall be permitted to speak, which means that God is to be permitted to *continue* to speak as He began to speak to me during my spiritual awakening, *against* my will.

The true and simple prayer of the penitent is therefore this: "Lord, speak; thy servant heareth!"

This is the right attitude of a sinner toward God! Thus do I acknowledge that I do not even know the will of God. I must let God Himself make it known to my God-forsaken soul.

Now I acknowledge that it is God's speaking, God's creative word alone, that can remove my animosity toward God and bring forth within me a willing spirit.

Now I want to hear everything that God has to say about my *past* life. I now desire to know *His* opinion, *His* judgment; I would rely no longer upon my own, nor upon that of my fellow men in general.

I now desire also to know His plans with regard to my future: to know the things He would take *out* of my life as well as the things He would put *into* my life.

I have now chosen the God-directed life, and deliberately passed judgment upon the self-guided life which I have lived hitherto.

He who has made this choice and has prayed this prayer: "Speak, Lord; thy servant heareth," does not have much to rely upon for support to begin with, not much joy, peace, assurance, or power. But one thing he does have, and that is a strong position. Regardless of the accusations that are raised against him from his past life, from his present life, from his hard heart or his divided will, he pauses in silence and makes this plea before a high and holy God: "I have asked Thee to speak, saying that I would hear; I thank Thee that Thou speakest to me in such a way that I not only hear but also tremble. And I pray again: 'Speak, Lord; Thy servant heareth.' "

It is not pleasant to be in this position, even less pleasant to pray thus. But then, such a person is also through "playing religion." To him religion is now a matter of life and death.

## 3. During Faith's Early Struggles

The experiences of awakened souls vary somewhat. Some are plunged into violent spiritual struggles at once. They would so much like to believe and have peace with God. But they do not succeed. It seems as though they cannot succeed in anything. They cannot pray right, not read the Word of God and derive any spiritual benefit from it, not be as sorry for sin as they should, not be really turned away from their former manner of living as they should, and not gain peace and assurance, though they put forth the most energetic efforts of which they are capable.

Then there are other awakened souls who almost immediately attain to joy and assurance. They are very bold and active, and to their sad-hearted friends they become a shining ideal—and source of despair. "Why do not I attain to the peace and joy which these people have received?" they ask. "Have I erred in some way? Or is it insincerity on my part that hinders God from imparting to me the gift of salvation?"

However, before very long these rejoicing souls exper-

ience that "the bridegroom is taken away from them."
Then their joy, too, comes to an end, "and then will they
fast in that day" (Mark 2:19-20). That is, now they
experience the same sorrow and distress as the others did
from the very beginning.

When the Christians in the days of Hans Nielsen
Hauge discussed this difference between awakened souls,
they expressed themselves about as follows: The conver-
sion-struggle is always a *death-struggle*. But there are
souls that the Lord cannot plunge into this grievous death-
struggle at once. To help them, especially to help them
not to despair, He gives them in the beginning grace that
they can *feel,* in order thereby to strengthen them for the
struggles through which they must eventually pass. The
Christians of the older generation called this felt grace
"the first kisses and embraces." These were what the
prodigal son received immediately upon returning to his
father's house, even before the ring was put on his finger
and the shoes on his feet, and he was given a place at the
feast.

Why does God do things in this way?

Why does He not give these sincere, seeking, groping,
sighing and anxious souls at once the peace, assurance,
and joy which Jesus has won for them and which they
seek so earnestly, in fact, which it is also the Lord's good
pleasure to give to poor sinners?

Thus many of these souls, who have not found peace
and joy, ask, now humbly and yielded, now rebelliously
and complainingly, as they look to a silent and inscrutable
God. No doubt many ask even after they have had the
experience of being made free by Christ: "Why did God
permit me to remain in doubt, fear, and uncertainty as
long as He did?"

Now, I am not one of those who think that it is possible for us to receive an answer to all the questions that

we might ask. However, God deals righteously and kindly with me even though I cannot *understand* Him.

But here I seem to perceive faintly an answer. It is
the *obedience* of faith that God is trying to bring forth in
this dark and distressing period. But if He is to succeed
in this, He must first reveal to me the disobedience and
*wilfulness* which still flourish in me, and that in the very
presence of God. I have turned to God, surrendered to
Him with my sin and my guilt, and this I have done in
all sincerity.

But behold how wilfulness, unacknowledged and unrestrained, follows me into the very presence of God.
Though I have acknowledged that I have offended against
God and am deserving of death, nevertheless I present
myself before God with *demands* all of my own. It is as
though I would say: "I have now turned unto God, and
therefore God *must* give me peace and assurance. And
this He must do *at once*."—And if He does not do it, I
feel almost offended!

The Scriptures tell us that God *kills* before He makes
alive (Deuteronomy 32:39). Only he who is willing to
lose his life, his old self-life, shall find life (Matthew
10:39). "The commandment, . . . this I found to be unto
*death*," says Paul in Romans 7:10.

As a matter of fact, God "kills" the last vestige of my
inbred self-confidence and wilfulness by the simple expedient of not giving me, during faith's early period of
stress, grace which can be *felt*, which I so intensely desire.

Here is the cross-roads which divides awakened souls
into various groups.

Some give up everything entirely. They heeded the
call of God for the sake of their own well-being, in order
to avoid unpleasantness. It was not really *God* but His
*gifts* that they sought with all their godliness. And when

they could not attain to the well-being which they sought, they lost all interest.

Then there are others who persevere. They do not return to the world. Nor do they get any farther than they are. They stop at the crucial stage. And really do not care to go any farther. They take it for granted that what they have is Christianity. Have not also others recognized them as Christians!

Theirs is not a happy lot; they have neither peace nor assurance. True, they say, but do not Christians have struggles and doubts! And is it not written that we should work out our salvation with fear and trembling! Thus they struggle along from day to day, and placate their consciences by their praying, their reading of the Bible, and their faithfulness in the performance of Christian tasks.

Then there are those awakened souls who do not go back to the world, but who do not settle down to the self-justifying efforts that I have mentioned above either. They seek *God,* not merely His gifts. And they admit openly to themselves that they have not *found* God, notwithstanding all their *seeking.*

Behold here how the Lord brings forth the *obedience* of faith. Let us meanwhile take a look at the *faith* of this unhappy and doubting soul. An older generation of Christians said: "To believe is to come to Christ with one's sins." This is Biblical, for it is written: "If we confess our sins, he is faithful and righteous to forgive us our sins, and to cleanse us from all unrighteousness" (I John 1:9). He who *confesses* his sins, therefore, has faith enough to receive the forgiveness of sins. In other words, he is *saved.* But he does not have assurance as yet.

This kind of faith was called in times past a *longing faith.* And this was a happy expression; for it is longing that characterizes faith during this period. This is faith's first and its determining period of growth. Faith is there, but as yet it is not mature and full-grown. Its immaturity is shown by the fact that it is still characterized more by longing, hoping, groping, doubting, sighing, weeping, and fearing than by happiness, security, assurance and peace.

And it is precisely this which begets the *obedience* of faith.

An honest soul such as this acknowledges before himself and before God that he does not have assurance. He complains often, and even murmurs against God, but admits this also. He tries to cling to the Word, the "bare" Word, without any felt grace. Now and then he succeeds, but more often not. Still he continues to believe, that is, come to Christ with his sins. It makes no difference how impossible it is for him to understand God's ways of dealing with him. He says with Asaph: "My flesh and my heart faileth; but God is the strength of my heart and my portion for ever" (Psalm 73:26).

And little by little this sincere soul learns life's most difficult art: to *surrender oneself fully* to God.

In many parts of our country it is said of a person who has become converted: he has surrendered to God. It is an excellent expression. But let us note what it means. To surrender oneself in war, for instance, means to lay down all one's weapons and raise one's hands aloft in order to show that one neither has nor intends to use any weapons any more. Then one delivers himself over to the mercy of the other unconditionally.

Note, now, that this is just what faith's early struggle has taught this awakened soul. He says to God: "Do unto me as Thou wilt. I have nothing to *demand* of Thee. Thou knowest how I long for assurance, but do as Thou seest best also in this respect. Give me assurance, if and when and as Thou wilt. I will cling to Thee always, and will keep close to Thy cross, regardless of how great the

pains and the struggles and the anxiety may be which
Thou sendest me."

Note now what faith in God is present, note what obedience, what submission to God and His inscrutable will.
I might be tempted to use the paradoxical expression:
never is the confidence and obedience of faith greater than
when the sinner believes in God without as yet having
attained to assurance.

## 4. At the Time of Assurance

Up to this time we have spoken of the strained, sighing,
complaining, weeping, fearing, and doubting type of obedience. With assurance, God transforms this into a *willing* and *joyful* obedience.

As it is the Spirit of God who gives us faith, so it is He,
too, who gives us assurance. We are already sons of God
by *faith,* says Paul in Galatians 3:26. We need only *confess* our sins, says John. And because ye are sons, God
has sent the Spirit of His Son into our hearts, which
cries, "Abba, Father!" (Galatians 4:6.) This is assurance. And this is imparted to us by the Spirit who is sent
into our hearts. This gift we receive *because* we already
are sons, it says. That is, not *in order* that we may become
sons.

With this gift of the Spirit, which is not the one which
makes us God's children, but which we receive because
we already are the sons of God by faith, we receive new
*light* on the grace of God. We already *have* grace, from
the very first moment of faith. With assurance we receive
only *new* light on grace. The Spirit explains Christ in
such a way that it becomes clear to us that we do not
need anything more to be saved than to be sinners who
would not conceal or keep from God any sin.

Now that life of faith *unfolds* itself which *was* present
in the heart from the very moment of conversion, when

the sinner came to Christ with his sins. Now it unfolds itself as assurance, that is, as happy, secure, and unquestioning faith. But not only that: now the *life of love* unfolds itself also. This, too, was present in the soul from the very moment of conversion. For faith and love are *one* life. But as was faith, so also was love in this first period of development; it was in the bud. And in the same moment as faith unfolds into assurance, in that moment the seeking soul's *unhappy* love toward God unfolds itself into a *joyous* love.

"We love him because he first loved us," says the apostle. Also before we experience assurance our love is based upon the fact that God first loved us. However, we speak of our love during this period as an unhappy one because, while we believe that God loves, we are uncertain much of the time that He loves *us*.

Now, on the other hand, assurance has banished our uncertainty, and we experience the love of God with all the faculties of our souls. Like life-giving, warm, mild sunshine it streams down upon us, body and soul.

And now, in this sunshine, our love to God unfolds itself in thanksgiving, in worship, in service, in joyful obedience.

The miracle is now complete: out of a disobedient, unwilling, rebellious, and conceited sinner God has created a humble, joyful, obedient, willing sinner, in whom there is an inner constraint, an inner, powerful urge, to learn to know and to obey the will of God.

We could also put it this way: the obedience which hitherto has been essentially an obedience of *faith* now becomes through the miracle of assurance an obedience of *love,* though it does not on that account cease to be an obedience of faith. We shall now consider this a little more in detail.

## 5. The Dissimulation of Obedience

Jesus says to His disciples, "the spirit indeed is willing, but the flesh is weak" (Mark 14:38).

The believer is both spirit and flesh. A willing spirit, joyful obedience, has been created by God in his heart. But his unwilling and self-counselling flesh is still alive (Galatians 5:17), and constitutes a living and active part of the believer's personal life. And now this heaven-born, fine, and holy spirit of obedience which he has acquired is to be exercised, tried, and made strong through a struggle with his conceited and God-hating flesh.

Which is exactly what took place in Jesus' own life.

He was sinless from His holy birth, and therefore never disobedient to His heavenly Father. Nevertheless He, too, had to *learn* obedience. From the things He *suffered* (Hebrews 5:8). His obedience had to be put to the test, to ever greater tests. The Bible speaks of these tests as temptations.

*Our* heaven-born, joyous obedience must also be put to the test, to tests that become more and more severe. These tests or temptations spring from our daily association with our old flesh, which "lusteth against the Spirit" (Galatians 5:17). For our flesh retains its old *enmity* against God and its *mistrust* of Him. And now the apostle says that it lusteth against the Spirit. It is a matter of life and death, a vital necessity, for the old man to cherish lack of confidence in God, to have an unwilling spirit, and to rebel against His will.

This inherent, living, active lack of confidence in and unwillingness toward God acts as a continual hindrance to our new, joyful obedience, a hindrance which, we should note, is to be overcome by our obedience. For it is this struggle which is to exercise, prove, and strengthen our joyful obedience.

If we are to be victorious in this struggle, we must, in

the first place, be clearly aware of the *danger* to our newly created obedience which we have in our own flesh.

Our flesh's lack of confidence in and unwillingness toward God subjects our new obedience to constant *attack*.

Since it is not easy to get a happy and obedient Christian to commit a direct and conscious act of disobedience toward his dear Lord, therefore our flesh seeks to attack our obedience from *within*. It bores itself quietly into the living *kernel* of obedience and eats it up, without touching the outward *shell*. And thus leads the believer into living a disobedient *life* under the guise of obedience.

This inner *dissimulation* of obedience takes place in many ways.

As a rule what happens is that obedience is little by little shifted from the realm of the *heart* to that of the *outward act*. Whereas formerly the soul felt that it was the disobedience of his *heart* that constituted his real sin against God, now he gradually occupies himself mostly with disobedient words and acts. He is afraid to use slanderous words, but envious and unkind thoughts are permitted to pass. He is afraid of committing the impure act, but he tolerates the impure attitude of mind. He takes care not to permit his temper to flare up, but he permits inward bitterness to do its devastating work freely and unhindered.

Then he begins to do battle against his sins in about the same way as the average man of the world. With wise calculations he seeks to avoid those sins which would damage his name and reputation outwardly or perhaps make his home life difficult.

The obedience of *faith* has given place to the obedience of the *flesh*. For the flesh also can be obedient, in fact, be very punctual in its obedience, if it can only avoid being obedient *to God*. If it can only be permitted to obey its

own moral requirements, or that of others, then it can be
painfully exact and remarkably persevering in its obedience.

For this dissimulation of obedience there is only one
remedy, says Jesus: to watch and pray. By that is meant
that we in daily fear of this terrible danger from our flesh
must keep so close to God that it will be possible for Him
to keep fresh in our hearts that love which makes sin a
thing we loathe, and which makes it a joy for us to obey
the will of God.

Can I reach a stage here on earth in which I in my
*heart* can always be obedient to God and never grieve His
Holy Spirit?

No, says the Bible. "For in many things we all stum-
ble" (James 3:2). "If we say that we have no sin, we
deceive ourselves, and the truth is not in us" (I John 1:8).

But I am to reach the stage where I am not satisfied
with anything less than the obedience of *faith,* that is, the
obedient *heart,* and where every disobedience of my heart
grieves me and drives me to the cross of Christ. There I
receive, in the first place, forgiveness for my disobedience
"through the obedience of the one" (Romans 5:19). And,
in the next place, my obedience of faith is strengthened,
so that I with new courage resume the gigantic struggle
with my disobedient flesh.

+

There is nothing that the old man within us is so opposed to as obedience to the will of God. Our old nature
will therefore do everything possible to circumvent or to
avoid the obedience of faith, not only in the struggle
against sin, which we have just mentioned, but also in the
*service* and the *work* of the Lord.

If our old nature can only avoid obeying God, it is
willing to make great sacrifices and exertions, preferably

if it can perform these self-chosen sacrifices under the appearance of doing the will of *God*.

Think of the Pharisees, how zealous they were in fulfilling their own religious and moral ordinances, which were nothing but human distortions of the commandments of God (Mark 7:8-13). Or think of the Catholics, especially the monks and nuns, how zealous and persevering they are in fulfilling all their *human* ordinances, which for the most part are a distortion, a caricature, of the revealed will of God.

A fear of God and a morality which gives honor to man and not to God, have the full sanction and energetic support of the flesh.

On the Protestant side we have something corresponding. We do not believe that we can *merit* salvation through good deeds, whether it be prayers or alms or fastings or vigils or pilgrimages. Therefore we are not tempted to arrogate religious merit unto ourselves by these things. But our disobedient flesh has sufficient means aside from these to dissimulate the obedience of faith: by transferring this obedience from the realm of the *heart* to that of the *outward act.*

Normally, the obedience of faith expresses itself in acts of Christian service, of many kinds. But the most important thing to the Lord is not these acts themselves, but the heart which *loves* to do the will of the Lord, which diligently seeks to *ascertain* the will of God, and, when complete certainty regarding the will of God has been gained, seeks with all its might to *do* it.

This, however, makes for perpetual pain and annoyance to the flesh. Wherefore it resorts to devilish artifices. It casts a spell upon us, as it were, distorting our spiritual perspective, and as a result we begin little by little to emphasize the obedient *act* instead of the obedient *heart*.

Henceforth to *do* the work of the Lord becomes more important than the *attitude of mind* with which we do it.

If we have taken this first step away from the obedience of *faith* and into the obedience of the *flesh,* we will soon take the next. Having begun to place the emphasis upon outward acts, it next becomes a question of doing *many* such acts rather than acts prompted by *obedience.*

This satisfies the flesh. When it has deposed simple obedience toward God and has substituted for it its own self-sufficient and self-directed will, then it is not at all opposed to making sacrifices and exerting itself; then it applies itself even to Christian tasks with much zeal and perseverance.

We note the same in disobedient children. A mother asks a child to do a certain thing. But no, that particular thing it will not do. Meanwhile the child's conscience becomes somewhat troubled, and it can no longer sit idly by while mother works. So it begins to do *something else,* something that its mother did not ask it to do, perhaps even something that requires greater effort.

Our Lord has many such disobedient children.

He reminds them gently and quietly that He needs their help in the performance of some task. But, at the time, they excuse themselves, saying that it is not convenient for them to do so just then. Or they decline because they are not certain what the consequences might be. Or they refuse because they know only too well that the doing of the task may entail unpleasant and even fateful consequences. So they do not do it.

But instead of acknowledging their disobedience they follow the very reasonable suggestion which their flesh at once makes: do something *else.*

When the obedient *heart* is no longer the important thing, then to *do* something for the Lord takes first rank. And if conscience is still a little restless because of this, then to do *much* for the Lord takes precedence over all else.

Thus is born and developed that self-directed activity which so often fills the church of God with its clamor and makes the work in the vineyard of the Lord so unspeakably difficult.

This self-directed desire to do things, this disobedient activity, is a difficult thing to deal with both for the Lord and for His friends. It is my impression that it has scarcely ever in the history of God's church been more distressing than it is at the present moment.

Likely, the reasons for this are mostly outward. We are living not only in an age of *work,* but also in an age of *organization.*

This carnal zeal is not only an expression of the ordinary Martha-mind, but also of that self-sufficient and self-directed mind which desires to make use even of Christian work as a means of *self-expression.*

The carnality of this zeal manifests itself in a number of ways.

In the first place, even though these people are engaged in the work of the Lord, nevertheless it is done more with themselves in mind than the Lord. Regard for their own honor, influence, and power determines what and how much work they desire to do. They do not feel "called" to accept responsibility for any task in the kingdom that does not reward them in this manner.

In the second place, in their carnal zeal they do not only insist upon *doing* the things that they have chosen to do; they also insist upon being *leaders.* All, therefore, who co-operate with them and who accept their leadership appeal to them very much. And the more carnal my zeal, the less will I tolerate others who do not seem to understand that the most important work of all is that which I am doing. And since the work that others do will at least limit my work, I will be tempted in my carnal zeal to hinder others in their work.

Here we have the source of that factionalism which from the days of the apostles and down to our day has done such irreparable damage to the vineyard of the Lord.

In the third place, this self-directed zeal is so taken up with self that it becomes very sensitive and irritable. If friends and co-workers do not accord its possessors and their work proper recognition, they feel hurt and become peevish.

If there should be *several* such people in a group, the most important and the most difficult task that would confront the others would be to move with such painful care as not to give offense to them. Otherwise they would soon find one or more of these people out on the periphery of things, peeved and pouting.

In the fourth place, this self-directed zeal often becomes a flighty and incoherent thing. Regular, daily obedience becomes too much of a burden. However, they still sense the requirement. Wherefore they resort to *extraordinary efforts,* and make a solemn resolution to do something *great.*

And the thing that seems great to them they feel that their co-workers, too, should look upon as something great. And if the latter fail to do this, these people become impatient. If inclined to be choleric, they push matters through by being insistent and applying *pressure.* To wait until the others have become *convinced* of the greatness of the matter in question, they have neither the time nor the patience. And they are even less concerned about resorting to *prayer* as a means of advancing their cause.

+

There are Christian young people living at home with their parents, where they may be needed very much to help with the work. These young people, because they have experienced the new birth, have become imbued with a desire to do something for God. But that they can serve God by being willing and conscientious workers at home with their parents, is not easy for them to see.

This is not entirely their own fault. We older Christians are largely to blame for this. It is easy for us, like the Catholics, to look upon work done for the Lord as something *extra,* something which we are to do *aside* from our daily work. We overlook the fact that our regular daily work constitutes the major portion of the work we are to do for the Lord.

If we will do *this* work *for the Lord,* then our daily life will become a daily *service unto God.* And, in the second place, it will become a means of exercising ourselves daily in the obedience of faith.

Yea, verily, in the obedience of *faith!* For this kind of work seems unimportant and drab, and no one pays any particular attention to it. Only faith is able to look upon it as a *sacred* task, as work done for the Lord. What besides faith can make a person understand how much seemingly insignificant work can be of any importance to the Lord and to His great kingdom?

But should not a Christian do something *extra,* something *aside* from his daily calling?

Yes, he should, and he will. It is the nature of love to desire to do as much as possible for the loved one. The mistake is made when we think that it is *only* the extra work that is work for the Lord.

Here, too, the example of Jesus is our perfect guide.

Up to His thirtieth year Jesus was occupied continuously with His earthly calling, as an apprentice to His father, who was a carpenter. This, too, He did because it was the will of His heavenly Father. Thus He *sanctified* our simple earthly tasks, and showed us that by such tasks we could serve and honor God.

To Jesus these years of manual labor were also, without question, a period of school in obedience.

He knew that He had been called to do the greatest work ever entrusted to any man: to save the race and to found the kingdom of God. And still He continued to live in Nazareth as a builder! He was now thirty years old, and still He had not entered upon His real work! The tempter most certainly did not forget to speak to Him about this. Perhaps to His mother also, who knew what His mission was. Still Jesus continued to live and work in obscurity. Perhaps it was not the first time, the time at the wedding in Cana, that Jesus had to answer His mother: "Woman, what have I to do with thee? Mine hour is not yet come."—John 2:4.

+

We turn back to our Christian young people at home with their parents, occupied with some earthly calling or other.

They desire to do something for the Lord, and try in a small way to do so, either through some organization, the Sunday school, or meetings of various kinds, or perhaps by singing or playing an instrument. But to some of them these things really do not count. Progress is slow; things do not go well at all. Moreover, they are not certain that their efforts are particularly appreciated by the rest. At home in their daily work they fare perhaps even worse. They feel that their daily tasks are tedious and inconsequential. As a result they go about them carelessly and indifferently. Oftentimes, too, they are unwilling and fretful. Then their conscience begins to annoy them, not only because they have erred, but also because they feel that they have not used their time to the best advantage in doing something for the Lord!

In such moments a thought matures in their minds which they had scarcely dared to admit to themselves was even present: "I am not destined to do this kind of work. I have been called to work for God. The Lord has decided that I should be a minister." Another may feel called to become a missionary; a third, to be an evangelist; a fourth, a deacon; a fifth, a deaconess.

The great decision is made! What release! At last they have found themselves! They would not be disobedient to the call! The sacrifice has been decided upon! Happy and very certain of themselves, they proceed to the accomplishment of the great and difficult tasks which now await them.

Did these young people make their decision in the *obedience of faith* or in *self-directed activity?* This question is of vital importance, not only to the future of these young people, but also to their life in God.

Some may perhaps ask: Can there be any doubt that it is from God when a believer feels a call of this kind in his heart? Is not this precisely the way in which God assigns the various gifts of grace to their proper places? First He imparts to the believer the *thought* of some definite work, then *interest* in it, then *desire* for it, and finally *courage* to decide in favor of it.

Yes, indeed, that is undoubtedly what happens when God calls men to special types of service in His church.

But nevertheless the history of the church and of missions is full of proof that Christian people have felt themselves called to such service without being called *of God.*

This question of the call from God is a difficult one.

Moreover, as I see it, it is God's will that it should be difficult. These difficulties are important in connection with the obedience of faith. And therewith also in connection with the work involved in the particular call.

I always feel ill at ease when the young person who feels

called to a special task in the kingdom of God has not made a success of his earthly calling. It may be that he has been employed in a subordinate position and has become so weary and tired of it that he is unable to continue any longer. Or it may be that he has earned his living independently, but is no longer able to support himself and those dependent upon him by his enterprise. I do not believe that the kingdom of God is well served by having such people assume responsibility for its special tasks.

At least not for the time being. Even though they have the necessary spiritual gift, nevertheless, they are deficient both in obedience and in fidelity to God. He who enters upon Christian work because he cannot make himself *thrive* in a secular calling, has certainly not learned as yet enough of the *obedience* of faith. And he who cannot provide for himself and his dependents in his secular calling, lacks as yet some of that fidelity or that ability which is necessary if we are not to be a burden or do harm to the kingdom of God.

I know very well that there are, as in all of life, exceptions; and so also here. It is the *rule* that I have desired to point out.

+

As I have said, I believe that it is the will of God that the way to Christian life-callings should be narrow and difficult. In this way two things are gained: those who are not called of God, but who are impelled by self-directed zeal, will as a rule be frightened away by the hindrances and will continue in their secular calling, often with greater faithfulness than before, having profited by the humiliating experience which they have had.

To those who have really been called of God, the difficulties I have named will be an excellent exercise in the obedience of faith, and thus the best sort of preparation for their future work.

A Christian young person feels a call to become a missionary.

He struggles back and forth with it for a long time. Finally he makes the decision to heed the call. He feels it as a great *sacrifice* to become a missionary. The greater becomes his disappointment when he learns that every way out to the mission fields is closed to him. Either the situation in his own home, his health, lack of funds on the part of the missionary societies, or an over-supply of applicants may close the way.

It is so impossible to understand it all!

He has made the great sacrifice and stepped forth as a "volunteer," only to find that it appears that neither God nor men have any use for him.

What a young person does *then,* depends upon the amount of obedience of faith which he possesses. If it is self-directed zeal which impels him, he will become impatient. And though he may not murmur against God, he will most certainly direct strong criticism toward those who are in charge of the missionary societies.

This young person is a *voluntary* mission worker, but an *obedient* one he is not. At least not yet. But now perchance the Lord may take him in hand and teach him the obedience of faith.

It is very possible that the *Lord* has called him to do missionary work.

The Lord has accomplished His first objective, namely, that of securing the assent of this youth. Now He desires to *try* him, to *prove* his obedience. So He closes for the time being every way. He knows that the applicant's health, the conditions in his home and in the missionary societies will in His own time adjust themselves, but for the time being He closes every way. There are a number of things that the Lord must teach this young man, things which can be learned most easily before doors which have been closed to him.

1. The Lord must teach him to *wait*.

Obedience is not subjected to many tests that are more difficult than that of waiting. King Saul was able to accomplish many of the tasks assigned to him by the Lord. But he was not able to wait. As a result he lost his whole kingdom (I Samuel 13:7-14).

It is not easy for a young person to wait, least of all when he looks upon his task as one so great that he has dedicated his whole life to its accomplishment. "The King's business requireth haste!" Heathen are dying in darkness. He is young as yet, but the years are passing, and he is getting nothing accomplished of all the things that God has called him to do!

But God takes plenty of time.

He knows very well that time spent in waiting is time well spent. He is fashioning this person into His *servant*, His *obedient* servant, who submits to God and bides *His* time, *His* beck, *His* nod. The Lord is bringing forth that *faith* which strugglingly, gropingly, doubtingly holds fast to the call as it waits for Him who gave the call to open the way that has been closed,—in the Lord's own time.

Indeed, God takes plenty of time.

He knows that there is no hurry. We think that every-thing depends upon the *amount* of time which elapses; He knows that it is rather the amount of *eternal* significance that is put into time that counts. John the Baptist's day of work was in all likelihood not more than a few months' duration. Still Jesus says that none greater was ever born of woman. And Jesus' own day of work was not more than from two to three years though He was to save the world.

Yes, there is time enough for our work!

Our training takes the longest time. But we seldom have the time and patience that it requires. From the Scriptures it seems that the most important part of our training consists in *waiting* for the Lord's time, perhaps in living a life and performing a task both of which are lowly and obscure.

Moses was young and zealous for the work of the Lord and concerned about the distress of his people. And he gave himself to his task with well-meant zeal. But it was self-directed.

Things went wrong.

The Lord could use both his zeal and his will to work. But first Moses had to learn the obedience of faith. He had to wait forty years in the wilderness of Midian!

John the Baptist spent the greater part of his life waiting in the wilderness. And Jesus Himself—even He had to bide the father's time for thirty years.

2. The Lord must teach us to *pray.*

Now, I do not mean by this to pray in general, but to pray about our calling in life and our future. Without a doubt it is through the simple and persevering prayer of the young man that these closed doors will be opened. It is through prayer that this young man is to receive the gift of the Spirit, which is the prerequisite to his being able to do anything *for the Lord.* And it is in prayer that he is to make preparation for his future work.

To pray for one's future work is to "load" time with eternity. The fact that so many of us accomplish so little during our long period of activity, is due no doubt to the fact that we fire too often with blank cartridges. We do not take time to pray

To *wait* and *pray,* to wait in prayer, this in itself is a work that can be wrought only by the obedience of faith.

3. The Lord must *try* us.

When Jesus had received His call and, in baptism, had been endued with power for His calling, He was led up of the Spirit into the wilderness to be tempted of the devil (Matthew 4:1).

We, too, shall no doubt have our *wilderness-seasons,* with many and great temptations, as soon as we are called by the Lord to a task in His kingdom. With Jesus it was obedience to the way and the will of the Father that the devil sought to weaken. We must pass through a similar trial. The devil knows that a disobedient, self-willed servant does more harm than good in the kingdom of God.

The great danger before us who are called to a definite task in the kingdom of God is wilfulness, the desire to lord it over others, popery.

"Though thou wast little in thine own sight, wast thou not made the head of the tribes of Israel?" was Samuel's query to Saul. But when Saul became great in his own eyes, then he became disobedient to the revealed will of the Lord. And from that moment he wrought damage to the kingdom of God.

There is always a great inner danger connected with a spiritual gift, with our equipment for a special task in the kingdom of God. We see this in Corinth. No other church had such a wealth of spiritual gifts, but neither was any other so puffed up and self-willed. This we see very clearly from the two letters to the Corinthians that Paul had to write. The richer the spiritual gift, the greater the danger of lapsing from the simple obedience of faith and into self-directed activity.

Therefore they who are called of God and endowed by Him for some special task must take a *special course* in temptation and trial, and pass the tests before they are given an opportunity to make use of their spiritual gifts.

How gracious God is in His dealings with us! He knows whereof we are made; He remembers that we are dust. Therefore He sees to it, as I have indicated, that we enter upon our God-given work through the narrow door of humiliation and not through an arch of triumph of which we had perhaps dreamed.

During this wilderness-season there are many things about us that the Lord must prove. He must try us to ascertain what we are *willing* to do and what we are *able* to do.

A number of young men are attending a Bible school. They feel called to become preachers. They listen, study, and write. They work diligently in preparation for their calling. And this is right. But their studies no doubt often become dry and tedious. They await with longing the day when they will have completed their preparations and are permitted to go out into the work of preaching. This, too, is easy to understand. But the Lord would try them first, to see if zeal for souls is their impelling motive.

A number of them survive the test. During their student years they see and in a humble way make use of the opportunities the Lord gives them to help souls. Some of them, however, do not see these daily tasks that await them. They are occupied with their education, especially with their *future* work. As though solicitude for souls should await the arrival of some certain day!

A number of young men are studying theology. It takes a long time and costs a great deal of money. They work diligently and conscientiously. And look forward with rejoicing, in many a weary moment, to the time when their tedious student days will be over and they will be permitted to enter upon the great work to which they feel they have been called. But first the Lord would try these young men also, to ascertain whether zeal for souls was their impelling motive for taking up the ministry.

A number of them pass the test. They see and sympathize with the souls of men, first and foremost with their fellow students. They pray for them, seek to engage them in spiritual conversation, and in general seek to help them both temporally and spiritually. What pastors such students become!

But there are others who do not pass the test. Some think only of their studies and their future work, and have no concern for souls. Others see clearly the tasks confronting them and are often uneasy, but pacify themselves when their conscience reproaches them by thinking of the work they are to do for souls when they have finished their course and have been ordained. They no doubt passed their examinations, but not the "test."

Other young men are in attendance at a mission school. They have received a call to go out and labor among the heathen, a difficult but wonderful work, about which they think frequently, and the thought of which cheers them on during the prosaic and dry years of study which must pass before they are permitted to enter upon their great and highly cherished life-work.

But first the Lord would try also these young men, to determine whether or not it is solicitude for souls which constrains them. And a number of them pass the test. They work conscientiously at their studies, whether these seem dry or not. But at the same time they love the souls of men and live to help them, be it ever so little, only that they may be of help. They are humble of soul, devoted to their studies, kindly in their dealings with their fellow students, a credit to missions, and a joy to friends of the missionary cause wherever they sojourn during their student days.

But there are also some who do not pass the test. They are so taken up with themselves and their great future work that there is not room for anything else in their little souls. Everything they read and hear about fighting the battle of the Lord and winning souls they relate at once to a subject which is to them particularly great and holy: their *future* work among the heathen. This they keep in the forefront of their minds with great piety and respect. There is at last almost no limit to the amount of work they will do and the solicitude for souls they will have *then.*

If I were a student in a missionary training school, I do not believe I should dare to think of going out to the heathen unless I had received grace from God to win at least one soul for Him in my own country. Out among the heathen this work is much harder than it is even here at home. How could I dare to present myself for the work out there if I had no success whatsoever here at home. I cannot understand how a mission board could defend its use of mission funds in sending me out to distant lands under such circumstances.

+

## In the School of Obedience

Even Jesus had to learn obedience (Hebrews 5:8). It does not surprise us therefore if *we* must learn it.

As the life of Jesus was a continual exercise in obedience (see page 18), so also our life here upon earth is intended of God as a school of obedience. When we notice how little we have learned as yet of inward, true obedience, let us comfort ourselves with the fact that we are still in school and that we have a faithful teacher, one who understands us well, in fact, who is known as the *Master,* who not only supervises but also gives the instruction.

He employs two means in particular in teaching us obedience. They are temptation and suffering.

He puts our obedience to the *test,* that is, He permits conditions and situations to arise in which the opportunity to be disobedient is laid stumblingly and enticingly close to our feet, either in such a way that we by being disobedient may gain some apparently great and easily won advantage, or in such a way that we by being a little disobedient may save ourselves from some great danger.

Here we have much to learn from Jesus' relationship to Judas.

From what is told us about Judas it seems very clear that money was his weakness. We might have thought that Jesus would have sought as far as possible to arrange things in such a way that Judas might avoid all occasions of stumbling in connection with money. But to our great surprise we see that Jesus appoints him treasurer of the funds which He and His disciples had been given by good friends, for their daily support. That is, Jesus would *not* spare him from the test. He tried him where he most needed to be tried.

Things went wrong with Judas. And this might make us anxious and fearful when we remember that the Lord will try us also at our weakest point. But we must remember, too, that He will make both the temptation and the way of escape such that we "can endure it" (I Corinthians 10:13).

When Jesus permitted Judas to be led into these temptations, it was because He by His daily contact with him, His intercession, and His loving care for him was in a position to impart to Judas all the strength he needed to *endure* the trial. When Judas fell, it was not because he *had to* fall but because he *willed* it.

We learn something similar from Peter's history.

He was of a fiery, fresh, impulsive, and honest nature. But he was *weak,* cowardly, easily frightened. This comes to light clearly in his cowardly and hypocritical conduct at Antioch (Galatians 2:11-14).

We notice that it is this very disciple who was permitted to enter into the courtyard of the high priest that terrible night. To a weak and cowardly nature the situation was particularly fraught with danger. But even worse was this, that it was Peter and not John to whom the fateful words of the maiden were directed: "Thou also wast with the Nazarene" (Mark 14:67).

It was thus at his weakest point that Peter, too, was tried.

We have the same experience.

The Lord does not remove from us occasions of stumbling. On the contrary, He often permits them to occur at those points where we are weakest. And, like Peter, we experience disastrous defeats. At such times it seems to us that all our previous training in obedience has been wasted, and we are tempted strongly to sink down into the mire of despair again.

But if we do, it is because we are forgetting that it is the Master who is in charge of our training. Like Peter, we oftentimes learn more from our defeats than from our victories. In defeat a sincere soul is often given new insight into his natural tendency toward disobedience, and as a result is drawn closer than ever to his Savior, thus to avoid grieving His heart and dishonoring His name.

*Suffering* is the other means that the Lord uses to teach us obedience.

It is written of Jesus that He, too, learned obedience by the things which He suffered (Hebrews 5:8). It does not surprise us, therefore, if we, too, must go through the school of suffering in order to become obedient.

Suffering is undoubtedly God's best means of exercising us in obedience. The little measure of obedience which each one of us may have acquired in the past we have no doubt learned through the greater or lesser sufferings which the Lord has felt He could call upon us to bear.

We all have an instinctive fear of suffering. That is why our obedience is put to such a hard test when God comes to us through suffering. The believer must, of course, as all other people, reconcile himself to suffering.

But the attitude of mind in which he meets and bears it reveals to him the lack of confidence in God which is present in his heart.

He did not feel his lack of faith in God very much as long as prosperity and ease were his lot. He felt satisfied with God, and thought that His rule was just and gracious. He found no difficulty whatsoever in feeling grateful to God.

But now, when body and soul are being racked with suffering, now, when all his plans are being crossed by the stern will of God, it is difficult to give thanks. And now lack of confidence manifests itself. Why does God deal thus with *me?* My friends and acquaintances are all happy and well.

And if our suffering becomes great, either exceptionally intense or long, then our obedience is tried even more severely. We turn to God in our distress and ask Him to relieve or put an end to our suffering. We know that God need only move a finger and we will be free from suffering. But God does not move a finger. Our suffering takes its natural course.

Then, indeed, both our faith and our obedience are tried.

How can God act thus? Is He not merciful? Why then does He not relieve the suffering of His little, helpless child, who begs Him so imploringly to do so? But then, too, our trust and our obedience become the more valuable and the more precious in the sight of God, as His child humbles himself under His mighty hand and begins to sing in subdued tones:

> I would walk beneath the cross;
> Bear it with quiet joy,
> The cross, O Savior, which is Thine!

Then it is *God* in whom we trust, not His gifts.

Then it is the will of God that one loves, even though it crushes our own. This is in truth the obedience of *faith.*

## BLIND OBEDIENCE

This is the highest stage of the obedience of faith.

We call it blind obedience because it does not see or understand in the least God's plans or purposes in connection with the sufferings or difficulties which He sends us.

This obedience, too, Jesus had to learn. In Gethsemane and on the cross the tempter was permitted to obscure His vision, which was otherwise so clear, preventing Him from seeing the Father's purpose in connection with the unbearable suffering He called upon His Son to endure. First He prayed: "My Father, if it be possible, let this cup pass away from me." And when it was at its worst He cried: "My God, my God, why hast thou forsaken me?"

But obedient He was, and obedient He continued to be through it all. He added to His prayer for release the wonderful words: "Nevertheless, not as I will, but as thou wilt."

Here is obedience made *perfect*.

In this His deepest humiliation Jesus did not understand the will of the Father. In fact, He felt as though the Father had forsaken and rejected Him. But He was obedient nevertheless. To the will of His Father He submits, regardless of what the Father does. This is faith in God made perfect. This is also the obedience of faith made perfect. That this, according to the Scriptures, was the innermost and essential thing in redemption itself is therefore not so strange: "He humbled himself, becoming *obedient* even unto death, . . . *Wherefore* also God highly exalted him" (Philippians 2:8-9). "So through the *obedience* of the one shall the many be made righteous" (Romans 5:19).

Abraham also had to learn blind obedience.

His faith and obedience were put to many and various tests. He had emigrated from his own country and left his own people because God had commanded him to go to another country, which he and his descendants were to possess. There God would bless him, especially his *seed,* unto many generations. Yea, through his seed all the nations of the world were to be blessed.

But no children were born to him and his wife Sarah. And time passed; Sarah became ninety years old. We can perhaps imagine some of the trials of faith and obedience with which these many and long years were filled. Then by way of a miracle God gave these two superannuated people a son. Naturally their joy was great, and they no doubt felt that they had now received double for all their long years of waiting and trial.

But then something terrible happened.

When the boy was about half-grown, Abraham received another revelation from God. And the voice out of heaven spoke these frightful words: "Abraham, . . . Take now thy son, thine only son, whom thou lovest, even Isaac, and get thee into the Land of Moriah; and offer him there for a burnt-offering upon one of the mountains which I will tell thee of" (Genesis 22:2).

Incomprehensible! Unreasonable! Impossible!

First give him a son in his extremely old age, and then take the boy's life before he is full-grown! What would then become of all God's promises about the seed and the blessing unto all the nations of the earth? Had Abraham or Sarah sinned against the commandments of God? But why should the boy have to atone for this, and with his very life?

Now read the twenty-second chapter of Genesis, and you will see what faith in God is. Abraham is called in the Scriptures the father of all them that believe (Romans 4:11-12). The account here tells us what *this* cost him. Abraham was neither perfect nor sinless, but to *believe* in God was to him the same as to *obey* God. Therefore he obeys Him now too, without wavering, yea, even without protesting.

He takes "his son, his only son, the one whom he loves," and goes into the land of Moriah to do with him as the God whose ways are past finding out had commanded. In all the Scriptures there is not another example like this of unqualified obedience to God on the part of fallen man.

Every child of God will sooner or later experience the day when God will put to us the requirement of *blind* obedience. As mentioned before, we all have within ourselves an innate tendency to disobey God. It involves, therefore, somewhat of a struggle for all of us to obey God, even when we understand the purpose of His commandment and we see and recognize how important it is both to ourselves and to others to willingly humble ourselves beneath the mighty hand of God. But the temptation to be disobedient becomes many times stronger when we can see no plan or purpose in that which God sends us.

That He is past finding out is also a part of God's nature (Romans 11:33; Isaiah 55:8-9). He is so great that no part of creation can understand Him perfectly. Therefore no person can experience God without coming in contact with His inscrutability.

We can suffer many things with comparative calm if we can only see the *reason* for our suffering, or its *purpose*.

But the things we cannot understand, which to us so easily tend to become meaningless, irritate us and stir us to rebellion more than anything else. There is, therefore, scarcely any aspect of God at which we tend to take offense more quickly than this, His inscrutability. We are reminded of the rueful words of Jesus: "Blessed is he, whosoever shall find no occasion of stumbling in me" (Matthew 11:6).

But for this same reason, too, there is no aspect of God which tends so quickly to break down our self-confidence

and self-sufficiency as this. Here we encounter something
in the presence of which we are utterly helpless.

As long as we have not learned to surrender ourselves
to a God whose ways are past finding out, our whole
human personality will be in revolt. That which we cannot understand always fills us with paralyzing anxiety.
But he who holds out in this anxiety, without fleeing from
God and his own conscience, and who remains in the
presence of the unsearchable God, experiences a miracle:
God breaks down his self-confidence. Without being able
to understand how, the helpless sinner is drawn to this
God whom he cannot understand. It is God Himself who
in Christ enables him to humble himself beneath the God
whom he cannot fully comprehend, yea, even to depend
upon and to rest in such a God.

Like Abraham, we too receive word from God that our
Isaac must be sacrificed, the dearest and best that we have,
that to which all our hope is attached, perhaps that also
which we have received from God in order that we might
become a blessing.

To the sincere child of God, who is led by the Spirit
of God, the place of prayer is a bloody battle ground.
There in all loneliness he consigns to the grave many
cherished hopes, many plans and interests.

Jesus speaks somewhere about those who make themselves eunuchs for the sake of the kingdom of God. And
He adds these remarkable words: "He that is able to receive it, let him receive it!" (Matthew 9:12.)

A young Christian farmer's wife had the terrible experience one day of seeing them come carrying her husband
home as a corpse. He had gone out in the morning well
and happy, but suffered a stroke while in the fields. Now
he was being returned to his home, dead.

To begin with the blow almost overwhelmed her completely. She was in a daze for a long time. But her only

child, a little boy, became the means of gradually restoring to her the courage and the desire to live. He, of course, needed all her love and care. And since he was the very picture of his father, he became doubly precious to her. And the two lived a rich and beautiful life together for a number of years.

Then the boy was stricken with diphtheria. A physician who lived near by treated the boy from the very beginning. All went well the first few days, but then the sickness took a turn for the worse; and one day the doctor had to confide to the mother that there was no prospect of saving the life of the boy. Finally he expressed himself to the effect that it was only a question of hours. He would make a brief call on another patient, and then return to the bedside of the lad.

Then the mother went into her room and cried in her distress to God. The boy was the dearest thing she had on earth, the only thing she now had to live for. She prayed that she might keep her son. When she returned to the sick room the boy was asleep. The doctor returned immediately. He noticed at once that a change had taken place in the boy. And he admitted that he could not understand that the illness could take such a sudden turn. When the boy awoke after several hours of sleep, he was quite well, ate, played, and talked as he had always done.

The joy of the mother was indescribable. Not only had she been privileged to keep her dear child, but God had heard her prayer and performed a great miracle. A few days of exultation and joy passed. The boy continued to be well.

Then the thought suddenly struck the mother: "What have I done? God no doubt saw that it was best for the boy to die now. Perhaps this was the only way in which the boy could be saved. And now in selfishness you have forced your own will through, because you thought that you could not live without the lad. Suppose that by so doing you become responsible for the boy's eternal damnation?"

Thus she struggled for several days, vacillating between gratitude for the miracle and fear of having been self-willed. She felt that she had to give the boy back to the Lord, though it was like tearing the very heart out of her bosom. What would life be to her if God should take the lad? She could not endure the thought of it. So she simply closed her eyes, put aside her thoughts, and put the little fellow back into the hands of God, saying: "If I have in my prayers demanded that I be permitted to keep my boy, contrary to Thy well-pleasing will, then I pray Thee now: do with him according to *Thy* will, not according to mine."

Thereupon calmness descended upon her, and that night she went to bed feeling more secure and peaceful than she had for a long time. The lad lay by her side and slept quietly and soundly. When she awoke the next morning, the little one lay there dead, in exactly the same position as the evening before.

Heroic things are still done in all quietude before the face of the Lord. Nothing is written of it in the papers. But the Lord takes notice of these tremendous struggles and victories. And He will recompense, not only in His eternal heaven, but also here on earth. For he who would lose his life shall find it. He shall find life, the real meaning of life, which is to believe in God in such a way that one obeys Him: the obedience of faith.

# The Hour of Temptation

*"Simon Simon, behold, Satan asked to have you, that he might sift you as wheat: but I made supplication for thee that thy faith fail not."*      Luke 22:31-32

TEMPTATION!
It is life's danger-element. It is life's temporal, yea, eternal risk. Temptation belongs to the realm of the spirit, to the realm of the personal. There is no such thing as a human being not subject to temptation. There can be no morality, no religion, without temptation. Nor can character be formed without being tried in the flaming fires of temptation.

Hours of temptation!

They are the decisive hours of life. They determine the very course of our lives.

Between these hours life flows on calmly and securely, in comparison. But in the hour of temptation something very significant takes place within us, something very decisive in its importance, something vital to our whole being.

The hours of temptation are brief, but fraught with destiny and filled with eternal import. The course of our life, not only the temporal, but the eternal as well, is determined in these fleeting moments.

That is why the *invisible world* is so active in the hour of temptation. They up there know what the moments of temptation mean to us, and therefore they follow us in our temptations, not only with tense interest but with their own invisible activity.

That is what Jesus tells us in the passage cited: "Simon,

Simon, behold, Satan asked to have you, that he might sift you as wheat." Let us notice the *strong* expressions that Jesus uses: Satan *asked* . . . that he might *sift* you as *wheat*.

The thing that Jesus would emphasize here is the diabolical, persistent, and purposive nature of Satan's work. This is temptation's invisible eternity-side. This is what imparts to temptation a seriousness which far exceeds the significance that any moment of time can have, yea, which transcends in significance time itself.

During the hour of temptation hell reaches into time in an invisible manner. Here we have the source of the ever-flowing stream of temptation. This is what Jesus would seek to make clear to us as we walk thoughtlessly and frivolously down the difficult pathway of life, directly alongside of which runs the dizzy declivity of hell.

We have undoubtedly all felt, or at least had intimations of, these invisible powers of hell as they broke into the course of our brief earthly existence. Life's fun gave way to life's seriousness. We felt like a chip in a waterfall. In the mighty maelstrom of our *passions.* Or in the horrifying undertow of *events,* events which we had neither ordered nor anticipated, nor could control.—Events are more potent than thoughts or ideas.

Judas was entrusted with the purse. Peter gained admission to the courtyard of the high priest. And it was he whom the servant of the high priest asked: are not you, too, a Galilean? We have somewhat similar experiences. All of a sudden a combination of events confronts us with horrible tempting power. The most sensitive, the finest, organs of our soul feel intuitively that they have been seized upon by the cold, clammy hand which invisibly reaches out from hell to seize us. Even the youngest among us have felt some of this.

+

But heaven also is active in the hour of temptation: "but I made supplication for thee, that thy faith fail not." Jesus desires to tell us this also about the hour of temptation. Temptation does not only have a hell-side; it has a heaven-side also. From heaven are sent all the powers that are necessary for the defense of this poor little soul against the attacks of hell. In this connection Jesus mentions especially *intercession.*

This puts the hour of temptation in a new light.

An intense battle is fought not only *in* the soul of man, but also *for* it. This is nothing less than a struggle in which heaven and hell, God and Satan, contend for the possession of the immortal soul of man.

Jesus tells us this, too, in order to arouse us from our thoughtlessness. We live our lives thoughtlessly, as though temptation were a joke or a picnic, while they who are in the realms of the eternal take it seriously. And engage in a life and death struggle for the frivolous and thoughtless souls of men.

Oh, that the Spirit of God might arouse us to see the eternal seriousness and the eternal hazard of life. Then we would acquire some of that holy fear spoken of in the Scriptures (Luke 12:4-5; Philippians 2:12-13). This fear does not conflict with trust in God, nor with love of God. But it does conflict with the plans of hell, which seek to put us to sleep and prevent us from either seeing or sensing the eternal hazards of life.

"But I made supplication for thee, that thy faith fail not."

We have an alert and faithful Saviour. He follows the course of events in our little life. He knows when the tempter is laying his snares. He sees also how thoughtlessly unprepared we are. Then He intervenes, in order to arouse us and make us see and sense the danger. He will not and cannot compel us. But He does all that He can without violating the right of our own wills to choose.

A seaman told me that on his first trip he went ashore at a large foreign port together with his mates. The way did not lead to that which was good. They had already entered a hotel in which all the allurements of sin beckoned to them when he heard a voice which cried aloud: "Mother !"

In that very instant he awoke.

He felt the powers of hell that were reaching out after him. Without saying a word he left his companions and went directly back to his ship.

*Then* and there the future course of his life was determined.

He saw in that moment, not only the picture of his mother, but also of his Saviour: "I made supplication for thee, that thy faith fail not." That moment saved his life. Satan asked to have him, that he might sift him as wheat, and Jesus did not forbid Satan to do this. But by His intercession He transformed this storm-attack of Satan into the young man's eternal salvation.

+

In the hour of temptation our whole soul-life functions *abnormally*.

Sin is, on the whole, an expression of abnormal soul-life. For there is nothing so illogical, so meaningless, as sin. In fact, sin is the only meaningless thing in all God's creation. There is no reasonable ground for sinning, for violating the good and holy will of God. There is only one reason for sinning, and that is the evil will of man.

The abnormal aspect of our soul-life comes to light most clearly in the hour of temptation, both in our feelings, our intellect, and in our will.

In our *feelings* a flaming desire for the forbidden things of life is lit. For the moment these things seem more im-

portant and more valuable to us than anything else in the
world.

*Intellectually* temptation affects us as a weakening of
our powers of judgment. Not only of our moral judgment,
but of our intellectual as well. Our usual ability to judge
values is lost and sin appears less and less dangerous. All
the brakes of the intellect are disconnected. The most intelligent people can in the hour of temptation perpetrate the
most unheard of acts of foolishness, acts of which they in
many an instance must repent a whole life-time afterwards.

On our *wills* temptation has a paralyzing effect.

Our many good resolutions, made in the ordinary
course of events between the hours of temptation, melt like
wax in the heat of temptation, and disappear between our
fingers. Temptation renders us weak and feeble. We re-
semble a drunken man, who exerts himself as much as
possible to get up, but only succeeds in rolling completely
over.

+

In the hour of temptation even worse things take place.

We have what is known as *wish-thinking,* that is, thinking which takes place, not according to logic, but according
to the whims and impulses of our wishes. To strengthen
or defend our wishes we try to give them a logical founda-
tion. Much of this kind of thinking is done in daily life.
Without a doubt it is *this* which makes many of our
private and public debates so heated. It is not so much
the *truth* we seek to defend as our own wishes in the
matter.

In the hour of temptation we observe wish-thinking in
its purest form.

If our actions cannot be defended on *moral* grounds, we
become the more zealous to defend them on *logical*
grounds.

Then inner *dissimulation* begins.

That dissimulation of character takes place which consists not only in sinning when we are tempted but also in being false to ourselves afterwards. We lie ourselves out of our evil *motives*. We excuse the fact that we made such a mess of things when we were tempted by saying, not that we deliberately willed to sin, but that circumstances, other people, or our natures were responsible for it all. Thus we lie ourselves out of sin's deepest reality, namely, its *guilt,* the fact that I sinned because I willed to sin, that it was *my* act.

Here is the beginning of that dissimulation and prevarication, which, with Satanic logic, parries every blow of conscience.

+

The hour of temptation has oftentimes become the great *humiliation* of our life.

I think we all carry with us memories which bring the scarlet blush of shame to our cheeks.

We were unequal to the occasion. The metal in us was too soft.

We succeeded in longing, hoping, thinking, and talking, but not in *living*. For to live is to be *tempted*.

At such a time all who dare to look themselves in the face become terribly discouraged, especially the young. They are seized with self-despising, even with loathing of themselves. They feel that they are entirely unfit to live, that they can live life successfully only when they are not tempted.

Moreover, they feel that they are not only sinful, but dangerous and harmful as well, both to themselves and to others. They feel that they degrade themselves and others. They feel that they keep the best from coming to expression in others and bring out the worst.

+

At such a time a burning question arises in the mind of the young person who cannot look complacently on while he sees himself sink down into wretchedness and dissimulation: How can I gain the victory in the hour of temptation? This now becomes a question of life and death.

And, be it noted well, it is not now a question of skill and prudence by which to be able to counterbalance one's passions or to evade the dangerous consequences thereof. On the contrary, it is *victory* that one asks for now, ability to meet the tempter without yielding to his temptations.

To you who ask thus, let me say that twenty-seven years ago the question that occupied me also, to the exclusion of all others, was this: Can anyone tell me how I can gain the victory when I am tempted?

I received an answer, and am happy now that I can comfort you with the same comfort with which I have been comforted.

I would say this to you at once: There is only One, One only, who can help you. You may travel the world over, and listen to as much counsel as you will, there is only One who can help you. And His name is Christ. He has lifted old and young up out of the mire, and transformed them into holy men and women.

This advice is old now. But no new discovery has been made in this field.

Prostrate yourself before your Saviour. Tell Him the truth, how you have gone down to defeat every time you have been tempted.

In that very moment He will lift you up from your sins, up from the mire, wash you and make you clean. He will forgive all your transgression and cast all your sins behind His back. He will set you free! He will make you a child of God, for Jesus' sake.

You do not *understand* this. No, nor do I; but I rejoice that I may *believe* in Him who loved me and gave Himself for me.

This is the decisive beginning of *victory* over temptation.

For this victory does not depend upon your *morality* as much as it does upon your *religion*. This, too, is one of the paradoxes of Christianity, one of its *offensive* aspects. Victory in temptation is not dependent upon the new moral powers which we receive in the new birth. The new nature in us never becomes so strong here in our earthly life that *it* is able to overcome the old. Nay; "our *faith* is the victory that overcomes the world" (I John 5:4).

The world thinks that this is an unmoral doctrine, encouraging man to abandon himself to a mystical experience of God instead of exerting his own will to the utmost.

This *struggle* of faith and this *victory* of faith are also so new and strange to the child of God that it usually takes some time before we learn that it is by *faith* that we are to fight and win the victory.

This is also the reason why so many converted people, to begin with, become greatly distressed and anxious. They strive and they believe in God. Now and then they are happy, too. But as a rule they become exceedingly disconsolate; they cannot make any headway against temptation.

+

They have taken note of Jesus' counsel: "Watch and pray, that ye enter not into temptation" (Mark 14:38).

But to watch is a wearisome and trying task. Many are they who have become tired of it, and have given up watching entirely. Others have remained faithfully at their post, but have become weary nevertheless of watching over themselves and their sinful inclinations. The reason for this is that they have misunderstood the meaning of watching.

When an army pushes into enemy territory, it establishes lookout posts on every side. These sentries are not to engage the enemy in battle. They are to keep an eye on the foe and, as soon as they have established the enemy's position, notify headquarters, in order that they may prepare for battle.

It is this that *our* watch also should do.

We are to keep ourselves advised of the whereabouts of our enemy and give warning to our Supreme Command, that He may disarm our foe.

There are, however, many sincere souls who are unsuccessful in this. They watch and pray, but go down to defeat nevertheless. If my understanding is correct, this is due to the fact that they have not as yet seen the paradoxical, the super-rational, the miraculous aspect of the believer's struggle and victory. It is the faith-aspect of this struggle which as yet is not clear to them.

But it is in this very respect that the Lord is training them. And this He does, strangely enough, in part through the very *defeats* which they experience!

The holy art of believing is from first to last to allow oneself to be undone by the Lord, to permit oneself to be convinced, not only that one is completely bound by guilt and that it is necessary, accordingly, to yield oneself to the mercy of God and not trust in any merit of one's own, but also to permit oneself to become fully convinced of one's own complete helplessness in the face of temptation, and permit oneself to be rescued and saved by another, recognizing that one is unable to do anything else but to *allow oneself to be saved,* to permit the Lord to perform this *miracle.*

This struggle is called the struggle of *faith* and this victory the victory of *faith* because it cannot be gained by others than those who in faith have humbled themselves beneath God's mortifying grace, those who in faith have been willing to learn the lesson taught them by their defeats, namely, that they should give up all confidence in themselves and, like helpless children, stretch out their hands toward their mighty Deliverer.

This is the aspect of the believer's struggle with temptation which is such a great *stumbling-block*.

+

When the watchman has located the enemy, it is *not* his duty to give battle to the opposing hosts. That would be entirely useless because the enemy is so much stronger than he is. On the contrary, it is his duty to notify headquarters at once that the enemy is at hand. Whereupon the main division of the army comes and engages the mighty enemy in battle.

This is also our position in this struggle.

Our enemy is wholly superior to us. Our wrestling is not only against our own flesh and blood, but against the spiritual hosts of wickedness in the heavenly places.

It is useless *for us* therefore to engage the enemy in combat. Our new nature is not capable of overcoming the old.

Not at all. Our task in this unequal struggle consists in doing two things, two very simple things: in the first place, to be on guard, in order that we may know where our enemies are and recognize them as they approach us. In the second place, it is our duty to notify our Chief Force that the enemy is upon us.

Our Chief Force is Jesus Christ, who once and for all has conquered all our enemies and therefore can make us partakers in His victory every time temptation is upon us. And our Chief Force is not far away; He is at our side. All I need to do when I feel that temptation is approaching is to cry to the Lord: "Come at once, O Lord! My superior foes are here! Come at once and deprive temptation of its power, otherwise I shall be overcome in a few moments."

Follow this simple counsel which Jesus gives you! If you do, you shall experience the fact that this is not mere rhetoric, but a certain way to victory, even over your most difficult sinful habits.

When we are overcome by temptation, it is because of one of two things: *either* we are not wholly sincere in our desire to gain the victory, but secretly enter into a compact with sin. (Then not even the Almighty God Himself can help us.) *Or* the situation is this: We are sincere enough in our desire to gain the victory, but we have not yet learned to know our own helplessness in such a way that we cast ourselves forthwith into the arms of our Savior when temptation comes, that *He* may disarm our enemy for us.

This I would emphasize very strongly.

Temptation will gain the victory over us if we do not learn to turn to the Lord *at once* for help. The danger in connection with temptation is that it little by little distorts our perspective and weakens our moral judgment, as a result of which our view of the sin which is tempting us is altered little by little, under the quiet influence of the temptation.

As long as we are not under the influence of temptation we feel strong. We feel a distinct aversion toward the sin involved. But when we begin to be tempted, a change occurs, quietly and unnoticed. Our desires are intensified, our judgment weakened, and our will paralyzed, as indicated above.

For that reason none gain the victory over temptation except those who have become so convinced of their own impotence and incapacity in this unequal struggle that they, without attempting to meet temptation's power in their own strength, creep as a child to their Savior and say: "Now I shall fall again if you do not intervene between me and temptations."

How does Jesus deprive our temptations of their power?
In many ways.

It may be by a little incident, so commonplace that no one else notices it. But to you it is a little message from your Savior, enabling you to see things in their true light again. As a result, that which tempted you is no more.

Or it may have been a little word spoken in your presence. There was nothing remarkable about it, but to you it was a word directly from your Savior. At once you were helped.

Or it may have been a passage from the Scriptures which suddenly came to mind. In that very moment it was as though the siren voice of temptation had been stilled.

But as a rule the thing that happens is that the Spirit of God makes Christ manifest to the honest soul which is being tempted. He shows us quietly our wounded, bleeding, dying Savior; and at once we see sin in such a light that it does not tempt us any more—this time.

We have triumphed. And are thankful that we this time too could avoid fulfilling the desires of our flesh. Such a victory cannot be won once for all.

Not at all. We will never be rid of temptation. The desires of the flesh will continue to make themselves felt even though we experience the victory which we have just described. The desires of the flesh recur, and must be overcome in the same way each time. That is why Jesus says: "Watch!"

This struggle and this victory are not complicated. Neither great gifts nor much knowledge are involved. On the contrary, it is so simple that not even a fool can lose his way (Isaiah 35:8). It is hidden from the wise and understanding, but is revealed to babes (Matthew 11:25).

The more the believer feels his own lack of spiritual maturity and wisdom, the more certainly and readily will he resort to this way of gaining the victory, becoming so dependent upon his Savior that he feels prompted at the least temptation to cast himself forthwith into His mighty arms.

+

Before bringing this little meditation to a close I shall mention one hour of temptation which is very serious and in which much is at issue.

I refer to the time of *spiritual awakening.*

There are paradoxical elements connected with the period of spiritual awakening also which give occasion to stumbling. For the call of God, our spiritual awakening, is connected with a definite time. Our little intellect feels itself called upon to ask: Why does not God call a person at all times during one's lifetime?

I do not know whether you will ever get an answer to this question. But the Scriptures and experience tell you that the call is bound up with *definite* times, yea, even comparatively brief times in a person's life: "Seek ye the Lord while he may be found; call ye upon him while he is near!" (Isaiah 55:6.)

The holy time in which God calls you, the hour of your spiritual awakening, has been prepared by God for a long time, without your knowing anything about it. Prepared to the smallest detail. Prepared through events both small and great which God has ordained in your life, throughout every moment of your lifetime.

Then, when the preparations have been completed, God introduces into your life the sacred miracle which we call spiritual awakening: God draws you quietly into His holy presence.

But then, too, the hour of temptation has really come upon you.

For you do not feel at ease in the presence of God; you are afraid of Him. You would prefer to avoid Him. As a result this temptation comes to you : There cannot be such a great hurry about this. I will become a Christian. But just now it is not convenient. Later it will undoubtedly be easier for me to make this great decision and make it for all time to come.

This is the fateful temptation which comes to those who have been awakened spiritually.

Here, too, hell is an active participant in the hour of temptation. Why is it so vitally important for Satan to persuade the awakened soul to postpone his decision?

Is it because he would like to have this person as his servant for sometime to come as yet? Yes, that too. Satan can make good use of all who would serve him. He knows, furthermore, that a person destroys something that is of God both in his own life and in the lives of others as long as he lives in an unconverted state.

Nevertheless, his most important reason for having conversion postponed is another.

He knows what spiritual awakening means. He knows that there are only a few times in a person's life when God can call and awaken a person. And he knows furthermore that with the call goes a supernatural power, which makes it possible for the one who is called to break with his past life. He knows even more : that this power departs again from the awakened soul if he does not make use of it unto conversion. This power cannot be held in reserve.

It is for this reason that the Lord counsels awakened souls so gently and tenderly : "choose you *this day* whom ye will serve" (Joshua 24:15). "Today if ye shall hear his voice, harden not your hearts, as in the provocation!" (Hebrews 3:15.)

# Manly Christianity

*"Watch ye, stand fast in the faith, quit you like men, be strong!"*      I Corinthians 16:13

WHEN we speak of manly Christianity, it must be remembered that it has nothing to do with the difference between the sexes. Manly Christianity is as well suited to women as it is to men. The expression "manly Christianity" is, of course, a pleonasm, a super-complete expression, such as we use when we speak of an old veteran or a dead corpse. Christianity is manly, the manliest thing in the world.

+

Still there is more than enough *unmanly* Christianity, both in individuals and in Christian groups.

One encounters frequently something soft, effeminate, weak, instead of the strength and buoyancy of Christianity.

Or one meets something sighing, whining, and complaining instead of the brightness and cheerfulness of Christianity.

Or one meets something bungling and vacillating instead of the ruggedness and determination of Christianity.

Or one meets something unnatural and artificial instead of the simplicity and naturalness of Christianity.

Or one meets something frightened, shy, and servile instead of the candidness and lofty uprightness of true Christianity.

When we seek the reason for this, it is important that

we do so in a spirit of justice, which we do not always do. I shall point out two reasons which *explain,* even though they do not exactly *defend,* the types of unmanly Christianity which I have mentioned.

First, I would mention the *unaccustomed.*

We are all by nature *strangers* to the divine, and therefore unaccustomed to living in holy surroundings. For that reason we all feel somewhat uncertain of ourselves and move with labored tread in the presence of the divine.

This is not only true of our soul's inner relationship to God; it characterizes also our outward conduct, our words, yes, even our facial expressions.

It is in all likelihood true that there is no realm of human life in which it is so difficult for us to be natural as in the religious realm.

This, too, is a result of the fall.

In the next place, I would point out that much of our whining, complaining, and sighing dates from the time when our spiritual awakening took place. Then sorrow was natural. Any one who by the gracious enlightenment of the Holy Spirit has become conscious of his sins in such a way that it has gone through one's bones and marrow, will recognize that it is not strange if people turn to sighing and lamentation. At such a time there are undoubtedly good reasons for speaking of people as "long-faced." And I should like to add: I rejoice to think of long-faced people of *this* kind.

The mistake we make, however, is this: We allow this sighing and complaining, which is natural during the struggles connected with conversion, to enter by stealth into and to determine the nature of our mature, fully conscious Christian life. This is not natural.

+

Christianity makes people manly.

We see this best in Christ, the manliest of all men. He

was manly in the presence of friend and foe, manly in joy and in sorrow, manly at work and at rest, manly in suffering and in death.

I do not know what you would rank highest: the courage with which He spoke the truth, the courageousness of His acts, the courage with which He sacrificed Himself, the courage with which He endured suffering, or the courage with which He faced death. Here is harmony and naturalness, as there was throughout His entire life.

On a lesser scale we see the same in His men: Paul, Augustine, Ansgar, Saint Olav, Martin Luther, Gustavus Adolphus, Hans Nielsen Hauge, to mention a few the manliness of whose Christianity was reflected far and wide.

At the very outset Christianity makes a person manly. It imparts to men the loftiest and finest manliness there is, namely, the courage to recognize and to acknowledge one's sins.

1. Christianity gives a person courage to go to God with all sin and accept the great and humiliating *reconciliation* which He offers. It takes real courage to do this. How many are there not who have fled as cowards from this reconciliation all their life.

Christianity gives a person courage also to humble himself before men. If one has wronged another or defrauded some one he receives courage to confess and to stand revealed as the wretched deceiver that he actually is.

I heard recently of a new convert who, after his conversion, went about both in his home and at his place of business and asked everybody for forgiveness. He had not defrauded any one, but he felt nevertheless that he had acted in such a way that he should ask their forgiveness.

2. Christianity gives a person courage to break with sin.

Does that require *courage?*

Yes, *that* takes courage; because we all love sin. It is
our life. We are reminded of the words : to break with sin
is like plucking out an eye, like cutting off a hand. But
one receives courage to do this when one surrenders to
God and becomes a Christian. At such a time a person
takes up the battle openly against all his sins, regardless
of the cost.

3. Christianity also gives one courage to be faithful to
one's own convictions and to break with one's old companions in sin.

To break with them does not, however, mean that one
ceases to love them. On the contrary, henceforth one loves
them so much that one must tell them the truth; and ask
them to break away from the worldly and sinful life they
are still bent on living.

What courage is required here !

We are all cowardly. We are ashamed of being true,
whole-hearted Christians.

Strange enough, no one is ashamed of being a half-
hearted Christian. With half-hearted Christianity one can
be at ease in all circles and at all social functions. Vital
Christianity has always been despised and more or less
persecuted.

This is also one of the paradoxes of Christianity, one of
its *offensive* aspects.

This is one reason, too, why many people who have a
clear and strong conviction that they must be converted, do
not *dare*. They are afraid of the smiles and sneers of their
companions. Consequently, they put off God and their own
conscience with a little religiosity and an outwardly
honorable life.

Strange as it may seem, it has always required the courage of a real man to be on the side of Christ.

Most people lack courage to be in the *minority,* to go
counter to the current of things.

For that reason I would wish you success, you who by the grace of God have received courage to take upon yourself the reproach of Christ and enlist on His side.

We speak of *courageous youth*. That youth is indeed courageous and manly which is true to its convictions, its own convictions. And does not permit itself to be frightened or enticed into following the convictions of others. This indeed is an *upstanding* youth, a *noble* youth.

> "In the day of thy power, in holy array : . . .
> Thou hast the dew of thy youth."

Yes, youth with the holy courage of truthfulness, the sacred courage of their convictions. God be praised, there are many such young people even in our day.

+

There are many Christians who begin in a manly way, but who gradually sink down into the unmanly, the soft, feeble, cowardly, the artificial, the unnatural. Their Christianity becomes only a shadow, a caricature, of what it once was.

Permit me to mention some of the main reasons for this degeneration of the Christian life, together with some of the simplest means of avoiding it.

In the first place, we sin in our daily lives. It may be that our particular sin is that of a violent temper, or peevishness, or untruthfulness, or frivolity. Father, mother, brothers and sisters, children, and servants see it. Here it is that many lose their boldness. Both before God and man. They do not give up Christianity. That they are unable to do. But they become defeated soldiers, unhappy and unmanly. With the pressure of an evil conscience to contend with continually.

Their soul-wounds will not heal. They no doubt confess their sins to God, and try to comfort their restless souls with the grace of God; but peace and joy will not return.

The simple and unfailing remedy for this cancer of the Christian life is this: be manly, that is, *ask for forgiveness!* I mean ask the forgiveness of the people who witnessed your breaches of conduct. Ask their forgiveness. Tell them that you did not act like a Christian. Tell them how it grieves you. And you shall experience what great release this affords.

To ask forgiveness when one has done wrong is one of the manliest acts a person can perform.

That we all find it difficult to ask forgiveness shows how sin has ravaged our lives and made us unmanly. We all think, out of pure instinct, that we lose something worth while if we acknowledge our transgressions and ask forgiveness.

But in reality the very opposite is true. We are the gainers by so doing; we gain not only inward peace and joy, but also the respect and confidence of others. There are none that I have so much respect for and so much confidence in as those who have the courage to ask sincerely forgiveness when they have done wrong.

Pray God every day for this manly courage, and you shall see how successful your *whole* Christian life will become. We know that it is written, "God giveth grace to the humble."

+

In the second place, I would make mention of a weak and warped type of Christianity which we might designate as lone man's Christianity.

There are some who live in sincere fellowship with God, but who lack courage really to enter into fellowship with the saints. They are reserved and cautious, fearful lest they make mistakes. They are present, of course, when the saints gather for prayer and discussion of Christian themes; but they are silent, and are *determined* to be silent. Oftentimes they are extremely critical of those who take part in prayer and testimony. And the reason for their silence and passive attitude is that they desire to avoid criticism.

As a rule these people do not have the courage to admit this, but excuse it and dress it up as best they can. They generally hide behind the excuse that they are *spiritually modest*.

They look upon it as being spiritually immodest to speak out about holy things. Would one not desecrate and defile one's finest and most holy experiences by thus spreading them out before the gaze of the inquisitive multitude?

It is true that we do, unfortunately, encounter a type of Christianity which is immodest, we might even say unchaste, now and then. This type finds a perverted joy in baring to the eyes of all men that which belongs to the secret chamber or to the private confessional. But these mistakes should not drive us to the opposite extreme. The one is as sentimental and unmanly as the other.

Let it be clear to us that we have experiences in our Christian life of which the Word and the Spirit say: "Tell it to no man!" We also have experiences which we confide only to some one individual or to a few.

But let it also be clear to us that life in God includes a large number of experiences of a more *general* nature, and which therefore not only may but should be shared with others. As it is written: "Go . . . and tell them how great things the Lord hath done for thee" (Mark 5:19).

The communion of saints cannot be shared and experienced unless the saints communicate themselves one to another, giving expression to the life which they have in common. "Let the word of Christ dwell in you richly; in all wisdom teaching and admonishing one another with psalms and hymns and spiritual songs, singing with grace in your hearts unto God" (Colossians 3:16).

Now, there are some who excuse their silence somewhat differently. They say that they have nothing to contribute and therefore nothing to say. They can speak neither of assurance, joy, peace nor victory. If they were to tell anything, it would have to be only about their struggles, their defeats, their restlessness, and their tears. And that, they say, is nothing to share with others, for must not a Christian testimony be one of joy and victory?

You are mistaken, my friend.

A testimony must first and foremost be *true*. In the next place, it should tell of the great things the Lord has done for you. And are not your struggles and the distress which you experience in connection with your sins a part of the great things which the *Lord* has done for you?

Speak straightforwardly about the way things are in your life, and be very willing to ask the believers to help you. This is good for you, and good also for the others. But be on guard lest there be a *false* note of any kind in your testimony. Many have permitted themselves to be tempted by their environment to relate in their testimonies experiences which they have not had.

Be manly, says the apostle.

Let us avoid sentimentality and exaggeration, and try to say in a simple and direct way the things that are upon our heart.

In many circles the strong words of the Christian message have been misused; religious language has lost its original significance. Let us in a manly way begin to work diligently and unceasingly to bring Christian words and expressions up to par again. This is as important for us who speak as for those who listen.

Finally, there are those who excuse their silent passiveness by saying that they will have to be *receptive* only, for the time being, and later perhaps they will have something to impart to others.

Well, there is no commandment which compels every one to give testimonies.

Moreover, I feel a desire to protest against the spirit of legalism which undoubtedly is seeking to gain entrance into certain circles and which seeks to *compel* every one to stand up and testify.

Nay, "where the Spirit of the Lord is, there is liberty," says the apostle.

I know believing souls who are not able to stand up and say anything even in a little group of believers, but who privately speak of their Savior both to the converted and the unconverted. And I know believers who have both the desire and the courage to bear testimony in a gathering, but who in private have neither the courage nor the desire to say anything about their Savior.

I feel myself becoming indignant when I see a leader in a testimony meeting press young people for a testimony, pressing them, I was about to say, with both proper and improper means, in order to make a success of the testimony meeting.

This is not only undignified; it is also dangerous. Let us lay aside all worldliness and pressure and prepare our testimony meetings in simple prayer. Then the testimonies will come voluntarily and naturally.

But, having said this, I would also say to you who find it difficult to participate in a testimony meeting: Everything depends upon your attitude of heart and your will in this as in everything else. If you have the *will* to enter into fellowship with the saints in order to contribute your little part, you will without question find a way of doing it, either by a prayer, a passage of Scripture, a song, a hymn, or by some service to the saints.

I would also say a little more to you.

It always costs something to enter actively into fellowship with the saints. You must give up some of your self-life. It is easier, more convenient, less dangerous, to leave everything to others. That is why our old nature always interposes objections when we are about to make our contribution to the Christian fellowship.

Do not withdraw yourself; follow the inner promptings of the Spirit. You will experience the fruit thereof in a manly, sound, and undaunted type of Christianity, which will be a greater blessing to those with whom you come in contact than you yourself realize.

+

Finally I would mention as a cause of unmanly Christianity the fact that some begin, little by little, to evade the requirements of true Christianity.

They began well.

God was able to overcome their old selfish ego. They surrendered themselves without reservation to God, and their hearts were filled with the love of God.

They began to live for God and their fellowmen. Refusing to take counsel with their old nature they gave themselves, their time, their strength, their means. Theirs was a manly life from day to day, whether they were at home or away from home,—a fearless, uncompromising following of Christ.

But then a change took place, during a time of spiritual decline, perhaps as a result of spiritual undernourishment. They began to listen to the tempter's words: "Spare thyself."

They began also to discover many valid reasons for taking themselves into consideration a little more. That was all that was necessary. Gradually they became more and more careful and calculating with respect to their own person. They took good care hereafter to provide for their own comfort, their own enjoyment, their own advantage.

Now, too, they would be Christians. And, of course, they wanted to do something for God and their fellow-men. But always after they had accorded themselves due consideration.

And if one begins to do this, one finds that one's requirements, both in lesser and in greater things become more and more numerous. The amount one has to give becomes accordingly less and less, both of time, energy, and means.

Thus it is that a pampered and distorted type of Christianity, of which we have so much in our day both in town and in country, grows and develops. It is a passive type of Christianity, which does not know the meaning of sacrifice and which affords its possessor neither joy nor sorrow, only that lukewarmness which the Lord would spew out of His mouth.

Would you hear my advice as to how to overcome this unmanly type of Christianity? It is this:

Enter into Christian *service* and develop a willingness to *sacrifice!*

Nor should you permit yourself to be tempted of your old nature to think of something great, in order that the world might see your willingness to sacrifice. Nay, be on guard against sentimentality. Be manly; assume responsibility for rendering forms of service and making sacrifices which are lowly and which attract no attention.

First and last in your home.

Do something every day that you are not expected to do. You will notice a surprised and happy smile on the faces of your loved ones. Try each day to bring such smiles to them all.

That will give your old nature a decisive setback every day. You will again experience the joy of sacrificing and serving. Your soul will again be filled with peace and joy. Not that you merit grace by serving and sacrificing; but as soon as you cease striving against the Spirit of God,

He will freely and without merit on your part fill your soul with the blessed fulness of Christian life.

There are many strong and healthy young people in our country. They have exercised and hardened their bodies by all kinds of athletics.

Christian youth!

Will you not exercise and harden your *souls!* The same apostle who says, "quit you like men," also says, "exercise yourselves unto godliness." And Jesus gives us a still more detailed bit of counsel: "Even so let your light shine before men; that they may see your *good works,* and glorify your Father who is in heaven."

That youth which hardens its soul against ease and comfort by rendering self-denying service each day will not only become a manly Christian, but will at the same time discover that the simplest way of overcoming sinful habits is to exercise oneself in loving service.

We have now for a number of years sprayed our lawns and pastures with weed poison. This is a simple and effective way of combatting weeds of all kinds. Love exercised in a practical way is the best way of combatting sinful habits.

+

Our unmanliness perhaps never comes to light more wretchedly than in *days of adversity.*

Then we quickly begin to mope and wail and give up. But it is such a time that we are really called upon to stand the test of life. It is then that our character should be confirmed and strengthened. It is then that our faith and our godliness should be established.

Look first to God, who sends you your difficulties.

It is not easy when the Lord places His mighty hand upon us. But look at that hand long enough and you will see that it is pierced. Then you will experience inward release, even though your outward difficulties persist, yes, perhaps even are multiplied. And you will see that the Lord always gives more than He takes.

It is easy enough to believe in God in days of prosperity. Then everything He does to us seems so obvious, so good. Then it is an easy matter to give thanks to Him for His lovingkindness.

Not until days of adversity come do we see how much of our gratitude was true and how much only sentimental phrases. Not until God crosses our most cherished plans and deals with us in a way that we cannot understand does it become clear to us whether it was God or the prosperity which He sent us upon which we relied.

Also a manly Christian feels the pain of adversity and suffering. And he is not afraid to tell God how it hurts.

But it is this very sensitiveness to suffering and unwillingness to endure hardship from which the manly Christian seeks to be delivered.

In the first place, he asks forgiveness for the lack of confidence which he at the time, while he is suffering, has in God and in His providence.

In the next place, it is his constant prayer that he may learn to suffer, that he may be manly and strong in suffering.

There are many such manly Christians among us. A number of them are bed-ridden the year round. It was adversity and suffering which helped them to attain that manly and free-born type of Christianity which radiates from their lives unto all their surroundings. Theirs is a magnanimity of soul and a strength of character which has a humiliating effect upon all Christians who are devoid of the spirit of sacrifice, who shrink from suffering, and who are sensitive to hardship.

+

The greatest joy that Christian people have in these dark days is that their young people are offering themselves willingly in holy array, as dew out of the womb of the morning. Willing to work and conscious of purpose, they are stepping into the ranks of their elders. This makes us exceedingly hopeful of the future of our work.

It is a joy to me on my travels to see so many of these fine Christian young people. The sight fills my heart with unspeakable thanks to God.

But this gratitude also resolves itself into a prayer: Lord God! Grant the younger generation the joy of being more manly Christians than we of the older generation have been.

# The Offense of the Cross

THE apostle Paul was the first one to speak of the offense of the cross: "For the word of the cross is to them that perish foolishness; but unto us who are saved it is the power of God." "But we preach Christ crucified, unto Jews a stumbling-block, and unto Gentiles foolishness" (I Corinthians 1:18, 23).

But the apostle Peter was perhaps the first one to feel this offense: "From that time began Jesus to show unto his disciples, that he must go unto Jerusalem, and suffer many things of the elders and chief priests and scribes, and be killed, and the third day be raised up. And Peter took him, and began to rebuke him, saying, Be it far from thee, Lord: this shall never be unto thee. But he turned, and said unto Peter, Get thee behind me, Satan: thou art a stumbling-block unto me: for thou mindest not the things of God, but of men" (Matthew 16:21-23).

The offense which Peter experienced is so typical that we must take note of its characteristic features at once.

In the first place, it was *well intended*.

Peter is clear in his own mind that these words of Jesus about His suffering and death are unfortunate and harmful to His Messianic position and claims. The people would never believe in a suffering Messiah. A Messiah doomed to die and executed was, to Peter's way of thinking, a self-contradiction. To die the death of a criminal was in his opinion a manifestation of divine judgment upon Jesus, incontrovertible proof that He was rejected and accursed of God.

Peter would now save the situation for Jesus.

He no doubt thinks, as Jesus' mother and His brothers

did once before, that Jesus was beside Himself for a moment (Mark 3:21). He is desirous of helping the Master to regain His balance. He would do so as gently as possible. For that reason he takes Him aside, in order that the others might not witness the reprimand.

In the next place, Peter is absolutely *convinced* that he has a right to take offense.

Peter does not doubt in the least that Jesus is in the wrong. Jesus does not understand for the moment what the Messiah should be. But Peter understands. He understands also that Jesus must be guided aright. And after what had recently occurred (see verses 16-19), it is he, Peter, who must administer the reproof.

In the third place, the offense is one concerning which Peter feels certain in his own mind and therefore one of which he feels that he may *speak freely.*

Jesus' words about His own suffering and death have not raised any questions or doubts in the mind of Peter. That was very natural, because the thought of a *suffering* Messiah was entirely foreign to Peter and his Jewish contemporaries. We might therefore have expected that Peter gently and quietly would have ventured to approach the Master with a question about like this: "You are the Messiah, and you know therefore how the Messiah is to live, suffer, and die. But *we* do not understand how suffering and death can be reconciled with the Messiahship, with being God's chosen Son. You have given us light on so many of the mysteries of the kingdom of God. Will you not now also enlighten us with regard to this mystery?"

But not so; Peter is not conscious of any desire to be enlightened at this time. On the contrary, he feels called to enlighten his own exalted Master!

+

Jesus' attitude toward the offense which He Himself gave is typical.

We might have expected Jesus to give some heed to the opposition which Peter raised, which was so well-meant and of which Peter was so certain in his own mind. Even though Jesus could not compromise with the truth, nevertheless we might have expected that He would have taken some cognizance of the hard-heartedness of His disciples and their slowness to believe Him, the Messiah, and the prophets. He had on other occasions accommodated Himself to their weak faith and reconciled Himself to much immaturity on their part.

But this time His manner is firm and sharp.

In the first place, He gives no explanation. He makes no effort to solve this difficulty for them, though He at other times had answered many questions and solved many enigmas for them. This mystery, the offense of the cross, He allows to stand.

Why?

Because this mystery cannot be solved. The offense of the *cross* cannot be removed.

The cross is a reality, the world's most real reality. Jesus therefore makes no attempt to *explain* the cross or *prove* its reality. He permits Himself as the Messiah to be nailed to the cross, and says only these words: "Blessed is he, whosoever shall find no occasion of stumbling in me" (Matthew 11:6).

Jesus not only avoids any explanation of the cross; He dismisses Peter so sharply that we have never heard anything like it before. In Peter's well-meant words, in which he gives expression to his offense with great conviction and self-certainty, Jesus hears the voice of Satan himself. And cries out at once: "Get thee behind me, Satan!"

The natural man's aversion to the cross is satanic in its nature and origin. This is the most important thing we are told here with regard to the offense of the cross.

+

Before the cross of Christ was raised up among men, Satan and his agents did everything possible to prevent the suffering of the Messiah and His death upon the cross. And as soon as the cross did become a reality, the work of blotting out the cross, of removing the offense of the cross, was begun with fully as much determination as had previously been shown in preventing the Messiah from suffering the death of the cross. And an energetic, sharp-witted, and persevering effort it has been.

Ever since the days of the apostles unregenerate men have tried without ceasing to *conceal* the cross, or, preferably, to remove the cross entirely from Christianity. The offense of the cross is the impelling motive in this herculean effort.

It seems that the *intellectual* offense caused by the cross was not felt as strongly in the beginning as it is now. It was its *moral* aspect which at that time was felt most keenly. Men could not reconcile the *cross* and *sin*.

Men felt that the judgment of the cross upon fallen man was too severe. Men, they admitted, were sinful, but not *wicked*. And therefore not *helpless*.

We meet this type of offense even in Paul's day. The Judaizers' requirement that the Gentile Christians submit to circumcision was, says Paul, a veiled effort to remove the cross from the Gospel. Paul preached that sinful man becomes well pleasing to God by faith in the cross of Christ. The Judaizers taught that God's good pleasure could not be gained except by fulfilling the law, that is, by *good deeds.*

So embittered were they at "the message of the cross" that they persecuted Paul from city to city, and spread abroad all sorts of evil rumors both concerning his person and his gospel. They said, among other things, that the gospel of the cross was not moral, that it was in conflict with God's whole revelation in the Old Covenant.

Verily, Christ crucified was a stumbling-block to the Jews!

It was the *judgment* of the cross upon the *good deeds* of men which was the stumbling-block to the Judaizers. They have here raised the problem which the Roman Catholic Church has been struggling with down through the centuries, to this very day.

Roman Catholic religion revolves, like the religion of the Judaizers, about the law and good deeds. But the Catholics, unlike the Judaizers, recognize Paul's gospel of the cross, at least formally. But this has involved Catholicism in great difficulties. For the *cross* of Christ and the *meritorious* works of man are as incompatible as fire and water. Still the Catholic Church has all along employed the most desperate theological artifices in order to weld together these heterogeneous, dissimilar concepts.

The great masterpiece wrought by Roman Catholic theology was therefore to *conceal* the cross, in order that it might bring no disturbance into the *"meritum,"* the personal merit, whereby the individual acquires the good pleasure of God and eternal salvation. The *sacrament* has now become the universal means by which the Catholic Church conceals the cross and welds together faith and works, grace and merit.

The Catholic Church preaches Christ, yea, even Christ's sacrifice for our sins. But the center of their preaching is not Christ *on the* cross, but Christ *in the sacrament,* in the mass, which is the Church's bloodless repetition of Christ's bloody death on the cross.

Here the offense of the cross has been removed,—by a masterly stroke!

For here the *judgment* of the cross upon natural man has been abrogated. Pagan *magic* and *mystery*-religion have been put in the place of the cross. The purpose of the union of the sinner with the Crucified in the sacrament is

not the unmerited forgiveness of sin, nor the impartation
of a new spiritual mind, but much rather the impartation
of value to the sinner's good deeds, making them *meritorious* and enabling the sinner by means of this merit to
*acquire* forgiveness.

This has been and is to this day the *Catholic* offense
of the cross.

+

Within Protestantism it is the *intellectual* offense of the
cross which has been most prominent, even though here,
too, it is the *moral* offense which is beneath it all.

At the same time as Luther was restoring the cross to
its proper place, at the center of the paradoxical gospel of
God's paradoxical salvation, work was started deliberately
to conceal and if possible remove the cross from Christianity.

We can trace this work back to the time of the Reformation.

The earliest beginnings seem to have been made in Italy,
in circles that had been strongly influenced by the Renaissance. By way of Switzerland we can trace this effort
further to the Socinians, to Deism, the Enlightenment,
Rationalism, and to such philosophers as Kant, Fichte,
Schelling, Hegel, Schopenhauer, and to Eucken in our day.

The aforementioned movements and personalities have
differed widely. But in one respect they are absolutely
alike: in their opposition to the cross.

From the most diverging viewpoints and by the most
divergent means, scientific and unscientific, they have tried
to show, not only that the cross is superfluous, but that
it is foreign to the essence of Christianity.

+

Turning to *theology,* we find that even more work has
been done.

Verily, how has not theology worked with the cross! We might be tempted to say: what else has it, after all, been working with? For whether it has grappled with the doctrine of the Trinity, or Christology, or the sacraments, the cross was always on the agenda for the day, because the cross recurs in all the articles of faith and is determining for all of them.

From Luther's day until ours, on the Protestant side, there has always been a group of theologians which with all their heart has desired to put the cross in its rightful place in our faith and in our preaching. They have not been frightened by the offense of the cross; they have rather emphasized the offensiveness of the cross, because they have learned from the Scriptures and from experience that it is the full message of the cross alone which can judge and raise up again a human soul.

But the vast majority of theologians and the great majority of theological works, especially in the last 200 years, have been at work *covering up* and *concealing* the cross, or *removing* it. And the offense of the cross has motivated it all.

We notice the same attitudes as we did in Peter.

The offense is *well-meant, definite* and *outspoken.* As Peter sought to save his Master in a difficult situation, so these theologians would save Christianity. They feel that it is in danger. People do not believe in it; men despise and persecute it. It has fallen into ill repute. And they are convinced that the cross is to blame for it all. For that reason it is their desire to eliminate the idea of the cross from Christianity; then Christianity will not lose its hold upon the people of our day, and the people will not lose Christianity. Then modern man will immediately feel, not only that Christianity is *his* religion, but that it is *the* religion.

This well-meant rescue work has been attempted some-

what differently at different times, more or less clumsily
and uncouthly.

*Rationalism* did it most clumsily. Without further ado
it cut out the cross, together with all the rest of the miraculous elements in Christianity.

The *Tübingen* school of theology also did it by amputation, but not so rough-handedly. They were of the opinion that it was Paul who had introduced the cross into
Christianity. They wanted the Christian Church, therefore, to give up Paul's theology of the cross and return to
the simple religion of Jesus, where the cross not only was
not found, but where there was no place for it. Jesus,
they said, preached the Father-love which imparts forgiveness without sacrifice, without atonement, and therefore without the cross.

The *liberal theology* of more recent date has begun to
realize that such a distinction between Jesus and Paul is
untenable. The liberal theologians understand that both
Jesus and Paul were orientated about the cross, and that
it must be said, in so far, that the cross was part and
parcel of *original* Christianity. But nevertheless they are
certain that the cross has no place in *real* Christianity.
It does not belong to the essence of Christianity; it is only
the attempt of ancient times to *think* Christianity.

The cross was, because of this, a valuable, even indispensable, element in early Christian preaching. At that
time men could not comprehend the nature of Christianity
without the cross.

But now that thought-garb has become antiquated. Now
the idea of the cross, instead of helping any one to arrive
at an understanding of Christianity is, on the contrary, a
hindrance, in fact, the greatest of all hindrances to modern
man.

It is therefore now the church's supreme task, through
its theology, to rid faith of its antiquated intellectual garb

and present Christianity to modern man in an intellectual
attire which is in keeping with the thought of the times,
with modern man's view of the world, his sense of reality,
and his advanced moral and religious consciousness.

+

In every civilized country, in practically every church
body, we now find prominent men who are vying with one
another in rendering this service to Christianity and modern man, that of removing the offense of the cross. Moreover, these men have, as in the Roman Catholic Church,
acquired much skill in doing this. As a result it is done
with great *care* and as *painlessly* as possible.

Their surgery is not as brutal as that of the old rationalists. They do not *say* that they reject the cross. On the
contrary, they provide a very honorable place for it, just
as they do in Roman Catholicism. They preach about the
cross, and they formulate a multitude of theories concerning the cross. They say the most profound things about
the cross. Those who are really clever in the use of words
and hair-splitting phrases even speak of atonement and
substitution!

But what they have in mind, and what they also succeed in accomplishing with all their words and with all
their work, is this one thing: to remove the *offense* of the
cross.

The cross is no longer a stumbling-block to the natural
man, either as far as his *religion,* his *morality,* or his
*thinking* are concerned, when the cross by means of analogy has been assigned a place among the other crosses of
human existence, even though that place be the highest
and most important of them all. To make the cross one
of many others is to remove its offense.

When this is done, it constitutes a denial of the fact
that it is God who has raised up the cross and instituted

His paradoxical salvation among the God-hating children of men. Then it is humanity itself, which, through its noblest representatives, above all through its acknowledged leader, Jesus Christ, has attained to perfect insight into God's giving of Himself in love and which, through the death of the cross, unveils, reveals, God to the world.

When this is done, then the cross becomes no longer God's crushing, annihilating judgment of humanity, but humanity's great achievement. Then in truth the *offense* has been removed!

+

If we turn for a moment to what is known as *apologetics,* we find an even more self-certain and outspoken offense at the cross.

About two hundred years ago Leibnitz wrote a theodicy, that is, a defense of God. Of course, it was very naive and innocent of the great thinker to call his work this. For it is scarcely possible to refrain from smiling a bit when one hears of a man representing himself as one who would defend God. Merely the thought that God needs defense is typical of natural man, with all his self-certainty. Like Peter, unregenerate man would step in and take charge of our Lord's affairs a bit, in order that He might not be put to shame entirely out there among those modern men.

Leibnitz was naive; he called his work a defense of God. But most apologists, both in ancient and in modern times, have done the same, have presented the same defense of God, even though they were too clever to call it a theodicy.

What is modern apology but a well-meant attempt to defend and excuse our Lord before the men and women of today?

The apologists bow very deeply and in all seriousness before modern man and speak about in this manner: Our

Lord was, to begin with, a little unfortunate with regard to Christianity. But you must be kind enough not to take this up in the wrong way. Both Jesus and Paul were mistaken, and that in many important points, when they preached the gospel. We know very well that you moderns cannot accept this antiquated form of religion.

We bring you tidings of great joy. After the Christian church's 1900 years of uncritical faith in this antiquated gospel, our Lord has in these latter days been fortunate enough to find some modern theologians who have discovered to a dot how many mistakes Jesus and Paul made in their preaching of the gospel. We can now guarantee you that our Lord will not be subject to such mishaps again. We are giving you the true and the real Christianity. This each of you can determine for yourself, as far as that goes, for we have entered into an agreement with our Lord that there is to be nothing in Christianity that modern man cannot accept as the truth, his own inner self being the judge!

+

One might be tempted to ask: why keep all this work going? Why do they not get through with it? When it has been proved as thoroughly and completely as the last generation of theologians has proved it, that the cross is not a necessity, why are they not through with the cross? Why do they continue unceasingly to fight against the cross?

Well, it is really not so strange.

Because the cross of Christ is a reality; and it is not only real as other reality is real, as Caesar's death or the battle of Actium. Nay, the cross is the world's most real reality. By that we mean that the cross, in the first place, is the center of all reality, the center about which all other reality moves. That is why men cannot get through with the cross. Whether they desire to do so or not, whether they love or they hate the cross, they must grapple with it.

All facts *speak,*—a mighty language, a language peculiar to their own kind. What the cross says is the mightiest message of all things spoken by facts, because it is the mightiest of all facts.

What does the cross of Christ say?

I do not mean now what men say of the cross, but what the cross says of men.

*The cross of Christ is God's categorical judgment of man.*

Thus the apostles viewed the cross, and thus they preached it. Men were totally incapable of establishing contact with God. They had both morality and religion, but they were "without God" (Ephesians 2:12). Moreover, they used both their morality and their religion to keep God away from themselves. *From* man there was no way up *to* God. This is what the Scriptures say from cover to cover.

*Therefore* God had to come down to man, become man. Thus *God* passes judgment upon man's sin and man's helplessness

So incomprehensibly great is man's sin that God could not save us merely by becoming a man. He had to *die* for us. A death which we cannot understand, a fearfully inscrutable death, a death accompanied by all the paradoxical pangs of being forsaken by God. With much crying and tears the Son begs to be spared this suffering. But the Father cannot fulfil His petitions. If the race is to be saved, He cannot be spared any of the suffering.

And what do men do during all this time?

They put their only deliverer to death, and thereby put their own signatures to the judgment which God had pronounced upon them. Notwithstanding all their morality and all their religion, they are such *enemies* of God that they cold-bloodedly put to death His Son, even while He is working out their salvation.

Gravest of all is the fact that it is the world's most religious people which, on behalf of mankind, is crucifying its Saviour, that nation which also had been especially trained by God through the centuries in a wonderful way, in order that they might be prepared to receive the Messiah of God.

The cross of Christ speaks powerfully also of *God*.

First and foremost of His *love,* of the mystery of love: that He not only becomes man and suffers and dies for us, but that He endures a paradoxical death, one filled with the hell-pangs of being forsaken of God. And that for His enemies!

But the cross speaks also of the *wrath* of God, His consuming zeal against all sin, which cannot receive sinners into His fellowship without *atonement,* that wrathful love, that loving wrath, which would forgive but cannot, and therefore assumes the punishment due the guilty one and dies a redeeming death on his behalf.

+

Is it strange that men are occupied with an offense such as this? And never get through with it?

No, that is not strange. But *this* is strange: that the cross really has been preached all these 1900 years. This is indeed strange when we think of how the cross has been persecuted by men and by devils during all this time, yes, of how prominent, capable men, both in Catholic and Protestant circles, have succeeded in veiling and concealing the cross.

Men take pleasure in certain quarters in our day in maintaining that modern man has been the first to really feel the offense of the cross. One does not need to have a very extensive knowledge of the sources to know that this is only a loose assertion.

We have already seen that Jesus Himself came in contact with this offense even in His own intimate circle. It was then that He spoke the rueful words: "blessed is he whosoever shall not be offended in me."

Paul observed it also when he began to travel among Jews and Gentiles with the gospel of the cross. He records his experiences in these words: "For the word of the cross is to them that perish foolishness; but unto us who are saved it is the power of God." "But we preach Christ crucified, unto Jews a stumbling-block, and unto Gentiles foolishness" (I Corinthians 1:18, 23).

Paul says that it was this very word of the cross which he preached and which he was determined to preach. That and nothing else: "And I, brethren, when I came upon you, came not with excellency of speech or of wisdom . . . for I determined not to know anything among you, save Jesus Christ, and him crucified." Thus Paul preached in all the cultural centers of that day.

Moreover, since that day the cross has been preached down through the ages, notwithstanding all the attempts that have been made to conceal or to remove it. This is in truth also one of the mysteries of the cross, that it remains a part of Christianity no matter what men may do to eliminate it.

Men may hide it as long as they desire, it will still be brought to light again.

*Catholicism* had hidden it well. In the beginning of the sixteenth century there were not many who thought it would ever see the light of day again. Certainly the Roman Church suspected no danger from that direction. But behold, *Luther* put it in its place again. Neither emperor nor pope was able to prevent it. And the cross revealed its power as of old.

After a while came *orthodoxy* and entangled the cross in so many irrelevant theological trifles that it was difficult for the common man to see the cross. But notice how *pietism* came and tore this work of man into shreds and lifted up the cross again both unto judgment and salvation. As a result the countries round about witnessed a great renewal of spiritual life and activity.

Then *rationalism* laid its smothering hand upon the churches and rudely set aside the cross. For a time it appeared as though the world was forever through with the cross. But behold, then came the *awakening* in the beginning of the last century in all the Protestant countries of the world. It swept rationalism out and put the cross back in its rightful place. The result was such Christian life and activity as has never been seen since the days of the apostles.

But time marched on. Rationalism gained entrance in modernized garb, as *liberal theology,* and began to teach heaven and earth that the cross was unnecessary. But behold, a practically unknown pastor in Switzerland, *Karl Barth,* restores the cross to its proper place again, and smashes liberal theology into so many pieces that scarcely any one will be able to gather them up again.

Notice what is happening in Norway. What does it mean that prospective students for the ministry come to the Independent Theological Seminary? It has been said that two-thirds of all the theological students in Norway are studying at that institution. It is the cross exercising its drawing power.

Or let us think of the *recent student conferences for the northern countries* (Sweden, Denmark, Norway, Finland, Iceland). At these meetings we have no athletic contests of any kind and no entertainment. Our program is this: the old Gospel of the cross in all its fulness, preached unto spiritual *awakening, conversion,* and *new life* in *service* for God at home and abroad. Do such meetings attract young people? And: do they attract *academic* young people? Come and see! We have had such conferences every summer, and they attract up to four hundred participants! How explain this? It is the *cross* which is again manifesting its quiet but mighty power in the lives of these young people.

+

Verily, the cross is the heart of Christianity.

And as the heart cannot be cut out of the body without bringing on death, so the cross cannot be cut out of the Christian life without resultant spiritual death.

But this we cannot *comprehend*.

There is therefore something about it which goads and irritates us. In fact, it is a stumbling-block to such a degree that there are only certain people who will not permit themselves to be frightened away by the cross, but who, on the contrary, cling very closely to the cross. They are the *publicans* and *sinners,* say the Scriptures. "Now all the publicans and sinners were drawing near unto him to hear him. And both the Pharisees and the scribes murmured, saying, This man receiveth sinners, and eateth with them" (Luke 15:1 2).

When Peter lay prostrate at the feet of Jesus in the boat, Luke 5:1-11, he had no desire whatsoever, we may be sure, to criticize or enlighten his Lord. On the contrary, he felt so unholy that he asked Jesus to depart from him, though there was nothing he really desired more than to have Jesus remain.

Nor did the sinful woman in the house of Simon feel prompted to criticize or enlighten her Lord. Without saying a word she prostrated herself at His feet, wetting them with her tears and drying them with her hair. She desired one thing only: to be where He was. She could not live without Him.

Thus it has always been.

All have taken offense at the cross save those who have paused in the light of heaven and have permitted themselves to be convinced of their sins. When they in the light of the Word of God saw the reality of *sin,* they were no longer frightened by the reality of the *cross.* They did not understand the cross; it was and remained a mystery. But they understood the Crucified One; never had it been as easy to believe the forgiveness of sins as when they took their stand beneath the cross and saw their Saviour give His life freely, as a ransom for many.

The Bible does not say a great deal by way of explaining the cross. And what it does say does not tend to solve the mystery of the cross; it shows both Jews and Gentiles that the cross is not only in harmony with God's previous revelation, but that it is the fulfilment and completion thereof (Romans 3:21-26).

It can, however, scarcely be said that it is this Biblical explanation of the cross which gives the helpless sinner consolation and peace. It is not the *explanation* of the cross but the cross as a *fact* which is so decisive in its importance. For man cannot be comforted and helped by anything else or less than by entering into fellowship with God and living in His presence. We cannot be helped either by explanation or enlightenment or by the words or works of God, but only by God Himself: only by meeting God and being permitted to live in fellowship with Him.

But we know that no sinner can meet God and live, Exodus 19:21; 20:19; 24:10-11; Judges 6:22-23. It is only on the basis of *atonement* that God can meet a sinner without bringing death to the latter, Exodus 24:10-11. The atonement in the Old Covenant, however, was only a figure, a shadow, of the cross, which is God's *real* atonement for sin.

Therefore we can say that the cross is the only point in all the universe where the sinner can meet God and not die, not be put to death by God's holiness.

Therefore we can also say that the cross is God's mightiest miracle, mightier even than God's incarnation. For by His incarnation God became one with man, yet *without sin;* but by His death on the cross He has opened the way whereby He might meet *sinful* man and become one with him.

As the whole of God's revelation is bound to the *Word,* so also the cross. It is through the word of the cross that it is possible for us to come in contact with the cross. It is for this reason also that the apostle says that the word of the cross is the power of God.

But at the same time the apostle calls attention expressly to the fact that he speaks of the cross "not in wisdom of words, lest the cross of Christ should be made void" (I Corinthians 1:17). By this he most certainly means that he does not *explain, defend,* or *give reasons for* the cause of Christ, but simply *preaches* it. For, he continues: "I, brethren, when I came unto you, came not with excellency of speech or of wisdom, proclaiming to you the testimony of God. For I determined not to know anything among you, save Jesus Christ, and him crucified. . . . And my speech and my preaching were not in persuasive words of wisdom, but in demonstration of the Spirit and of power: that your faith should not stand in the wisdom of men, but in the power of God" (I Corinthians 2:1-5).

We are quick to think that a sinner gains peace and assurance when he understands clearly the *meaning* of the cross, when he is able with his mind to grasp the *reason* for the cross. Therefore we try in our preaching to make the cross as *understandable* as possible to seeking souls. As a rule we do it by making use of the idea of substitution, placing before doubting and fearful souls a little piece of divine arithmetic. When we have shown that this piece of mathematics comes out right, we think that we have helped our doubting listeners.

Well, God is gracious, and accommodates Himself in a wonderful way to our fumbling and feeble preaching. And no doubt He can now and then help a sinner by means of such mathematical calculations. But I do not think that it is this calculating and explaining which brings a sinner peace at the cross.

Nay, most of those who come to peace and assurance at the cross are not particularly qualified to follow an involved mathematical explanation of the cross. And even though they had the qualifications, it is clearly not along such lines that they come to faith in the cross.

Such faith is not the result of *thinking;* it is born through an *experience.* Men do not gain peace and assurance by being able to comprehend the divine logic of the cross, but simply by coming in contact with the cross, by experiencing the cross.

It is the Spirit who provides us with this experience. This, however, He does not do directly, but always through the Word. And He does it in His own appointed time and in His own way.

Usually it takes place all of a sudden, but it can also take place more slowly and gradually. As a rule the Spirit makes use of a passage or a thought from the Scriptures, either from the Old or from the New Testament. He can also make use of the Christian testimony of ordinary men and women, either written or oral.

But whether it occurs in one way or another, a *miracle* always takes place.

Through these outward means the Spirit brings us face to face with the cross. It does not take place in ecstasy or in rapture. No; it takes place while we are in full possession of our conscious faculties. It is not, however, our consciousness which *produces* the experience; our conscious mind simply *receives* and *assimilates* the experience.

As a result of this experience we meet the world's most real reality: the crucified Saviour. We need only *meet* Him and the miracle takes place: fear, anxiety, doubt, and uncertainty disappear, and our soul is filled with unspeakable peace and security. Distressing restlessness and uncertainty give way to a peace that passes all understanding.

This the apostle expresses in the following manner: "The Spirit himself beareth witness with our spirit, that we are children of God" (Romans 8:16).

If a Christian were to explain this witness of the Spirit, he would find himself in a strange predicament. He possesses this assurance; indeed, his entire daily life is borne up by this assurance. But if he were to try to explain it on logical grounds or give reasons for it, he would find that his logic would be very inadequate indeed. The reason for this is that this assurance is not based upon logic, but upon experience.

A believer's assurance is not based upon his ability at all times to point out the Scripture passages upon which he bases his sonship with God. It is based upon this, that the Spirit continues unceasingly to make Christ a near and present reality to him. This takes place, as indicated, through the Word, but not always through Scripture passages which he can remember. The Word is *implanted* in him, James 1:21, and is a living reality within him, whether he sleeps or wakes, thinks of it or does not think of it.

The most incomprehensible thing in connection with this assurance is that it can be reconciled with the believer's daily mistakes, sins of omission, and transgressions. Most remarkable of all is the fact that the more the believer is assured of the grace of God in Christ, the more sensitive his conscience becomes, and the more clearly therefore he notices both inner and outward sins.

How then can he keep his assurance?

The power of the cross, the mystery of the cross, is the answer. Through the cross he is not only *pardoned* but also *judged*.

The cross pronounces judgment upon all of man and upon all men. The cross is proof that no man can do anything to merit salvation. It is the work of God from first to last.

Man has nothing more to do with this than to continue to decide whether he will *permit* himself to be saved or whether he will shut himself off from the salvation which God offers, accomplishes, and perfects.

Here again we come upon the mystery of the cross:

It is the sinner's *relationship to the cross* which determines his salvation. That means that it is *not* a question of his moral or religious qualifications or his own efforts. God's forgiveness and good pleasure are not dependent either upon the sinner's awakening, conversion, faith, or holy life, but solely and wholly upon the cross.

True enough, no man can be saved without conversion, faith, and a holy life. But these are not conditions upon which God loves him. On the contrary, his awakening, conversion, faith, and holy life are a fruit of the fact that God loves him and through the cross has provided a way of receiving him into His gracious fellowship.

This is what Paul has in mind when he writes the remarkable words: "There is therefore now no condemnation to them that are in Christ Jesus" (Romans 8:1). "In Christ" is the apostle's way of expressing the right relationship to the Crucified One, to the cross. He tells us here that whether a sinner is condemned or pardoned is dependent entirely upon his relationship to the Crucified.

What an offensive enigma to the natural man!

The good deeds of the believer do not contribute in the least to his being pardoned by God. Moreover: no sin that he commits can condemn him as long as he is "in Christ." As long as he is "in Christ" he is numbered among the saved, "to whom the Lord *imputeth* not iniquity" (Psalm 32:2).

Paul has also expressed it in the following way: "But to him that worketh not, but believeth on him that justifieth the *ungodly,* his faith is reckoned for righteousness" (Romans 4:5).

Here we are peering down into the deepest depths of grace, are we not?

The sinner is loved of God and is received into fellowship with Him though no change has taken place in his sinful nature. The only reason why the sinner is loved is that God loves him, loves him with a love which by the atonement of the cross makes its own way to its enemy. After atonement has taken place, the sinner receives God's forgiveness for the one and only reason that he is a member of the sinful race for which Christ has made atonement.

He does not even receive forgiveness because he *seeks* it. For when a sinner begins to seek God, then God has not only sought him, but already *found* him.

Behold, this is what the cross proclaims to the sinner as soon as the Spirit through the Word has shed His light upon the cross. And for this reason the sinner retains his assurance and his peace notwithstanding his daily sins of omission and his errors, and notwithstanding his deep insight into his own evil heart.

This assurance is based entirely upon the cross and the Crucified. "He is our peace," says the apostle in Ephesians 2:14. If we take our eye from the cross, whether we look toward the world or toward our own sin and wretchedness, our peace is gone.

Therefore this assurance is and always will be an assurance of *faith*. Assurance is really nothing else but unconditional faith in the Crucified One, that is, faith which, with the apostle, is determined not to know anything save Jesus Christ and Him crucified.

Here we also have the answer to the question which is so often put: how can I know that I am *in Christ?* To be in Christ is the same as to be *"in faith."* And to be "in faith" means that a sinner is so helpless that he does not dare to appear before God with his own life, but only with the life and death of Christ. To believe in the Crucified One means that I would be nothing before God save what I am in Christ.

When my conscience levels its accusations against me: that I do not love God, but myself; that I do not regret sin as I ought, but am cold and indifferent; that I do not sacrifice for God as I should, but am worldly and earthly-minded; then I bow my head and say: All this is true. I would be condemned if I had only my own life to present to God. But Christ is my life!

+

This sheds light also upon *our preaching* of the cross.

We have seen that it is the cross as a *fact,* and not the *explanation* of the cross, which, both objectively and subjectively, is the sinner's salvation. Therefore we should not in our preaching be too concerned about making the cross and the atonement intelligible to seeking and groping souls. All we succeed in accomplishing by so doing is to make the cross more obscure to them.

God is zealous of the cross.

There is scarcely anything about which God is so zealous as the cross. He guards this more than anything else. And what He must prevent more than anything else is that we minimize the significance of the cross or render it obscure.

The apostle Paul felt this very deeply. With full deliberation he avoided preaching the cross "in wisdom of words, lest the cross of Christ should be made void," "that your faith should not stand in the wisdom of men, but in the power of God" (I Corinthians 1:17; 2:5).

As far as we can understand, the apostle placed the emphasis upon two things. The one was to *preach* Christ crucified to such an extent that he says he did nothing else and was determined to do nothing else but preach Christ and Him crucified, I Corinthians 2:2. The second was the accompanying activity of the *Spirit* during this preaching. His one great desire was to preach the crucified Christ in demonstration of the Spirit and of power, I Corinthians 2:4.

How *much* the apostle put into this he expresses in a remarkable way when he says that the Spirit gave him even the *words* he should use: "Which things also we speak, not in words which man's wisdom teacheth, but which the Spirit teacheth; combining spiritual things with spiritual words" (I Corinthians 2:13).

Here we have the main lines that our preaching of Christ should follow.

We are to *preach* the gospel, the gospel of the cross. We are to preach the cross as a fact, simply and clearly and as fully as the Scriptures give us opportunity.

We are to preach the *whole* cross.

Both the *judgment* of the cross and the *grace* of the cross. It is likely that we have preached the grace of the cross and neglected the judgment of the cross. Thus the whole thing has become distorted. The grace of the cross can never be proclaimed in all its fulness unless the judgment of the cross has been made the background. And the judgment of the cross never becomes so annihilating as when it is preached and carried out by the God of grace.

It should be the sigh and prayer and cry of our hearts that the Spirit may accompany our feeble preaching with the demonstration of power, that our hearers may experience the power of *God,* who puts to death and makes alive, who wounds and heals.

We, too, have the promise that the Spirit will give us what we are to speak, even the words. Let this be our consolation, though it be a consolation with which only *faith* can be comforted.

This enduement of the Spirit is not to hinder us from *preparing* ourselves. We should make preparation, not only in prayer, persevering prayer, but also by searching the Scriptures and arranging our thoughts. We may make even *written* preparation. The apostle was assured that he would receive thoughts and words from the Holy Spirit also when he wrote. It is our reliance upon the Spirit that everything depends upon, whether we speak or write.

# By Grace

*"Good teacher, what shall I do that I may inherit eternal life?"*                    Mark 10:17

THIS question is as old as the human race.
It lies concealed in all the religions of the world.
And cries out more or less distinctly from all of them.

The young man who on that day came running to Jesus was only one of the many to whom religion has become a serious matter.

Since that day there have been many such young men and women.

There are many also in our day.

Yes, a particularly large number just at this time; many thinking, pondering, seeking, praying, longing souls.

Before they sought *life*. Now they seek, as did this young man, *eternal* life, that life which is not its own destruction, its own death. That life which does not destroy the finest and most precious things of the soul: the sense of guilt and responsibility.

+

The young man asked Jesus: "What shall I *do* that I may *inherit?*"

This question sounds somewhat strange to our ears. But it is based upon the religious language of that day. According to Old Testament custom they spoke of inheriting the land, Psalm 37:11; inheriting the earth, Matthew 5:5; inheriting the kingdom, Matthew 25:34; inheriting the kingdom of God, I Corinthians 15:50; and inheriting eternal life.

The thought was that God had given salvation to the fathers and that the individual Israelite shared in that salvation by virtue of his physical and spiritual relationship to the fathers. The young man's question had about the following meaning: What shall I do that I might have hope of sharing in the kingdom which God has promised our fathers?

As indicated, the young man's expression seems a little strange to us.

But it is excellent just as it stands. In the first place, because it expresses the mind of the natural man on the subject: What shall I do? The natural man does not see that the important thing in this connection is *what God has done and still does.*

In the next place, the form of the question is good because a profoundly Christian answer can be given to the question exactly as it has been formulated.

The question is: What shall I do that I may inherit eternal life?

The answer is: Accept the inheritance.

Even in probate court it is so. The heir does nothing to inherit but to accept the inheritance.

And the strange thing is that the inheritance *seeks* the heir. Notices are sent to every country and to every part of the world, if necessary, in order to locate the missing heirs and notify them of the inheritance which awaits them. We have all read notices of this kind, sent out at public expense, stating that in America, for instance, some one has died who has left an estate to such and such a person or persons, who need but notify the authorities and they will receive the legacy.

This is exactly what takes place also in the kingdom of God.

It, too, is received as an inheritance. All the heir needs

to do is to accept it. Moreover, in the kingdom of God also it is the inheritance which seeks the heir.

+

It is one of the profound mysteries of life that both fall and salvation, sin and grace, are received as an inheritance. We speak of inherited sin and of inherited guilt.

This is because God has created us as a *race*. This race became sinful in the very first generation. When the first Adam sinned, he sinned as the representative of the whole race and impressed upon the whole race his sinful nature, according to the law of heredity: "That which is born of the flesh is flesh" (John 3:6). No human being could thereafter be born into the race of Adam without inheriting Adam's sinful nature. Therefore, every person that is born becomes a sinner by *inheritance*.

But *grace,* too, is transmitted by inheritance.

Christ is spoken of in the Scriptures as *the Second Adam.* Reference is thereby made to the fact that He is the progenitor of a new race, as the first Adam was the progenitor of the old, the sinful, race.

The second Adam, too, occupies a *representative* position in the human race. When the first Adam fell, the whole race fell in him. When the Second Adam lived His sinless life and died His redeeming death, it was the race which in Him atoned for its guilt. In its Second Adam the human race made atonement to God for the fall which took place in the first Adam. "One died for all, therefore all died" (II Corinthians 5:14).

From now on *two sets of inheritance laws* are in effect. As no human being can be born without being born into the race which was made sinful by the first Adam, so, on the other hand, no person can be born without being born into the race which the Second Adam has redeemed.

This is God's *new covenant* with the human race. He

pledges Himself to give *all* the members of that race a share in redemption, which belongs to the entire race because Christ is the representative of the whole race.

Behold, here is the *inheritance!*

I was made a partaker in sin wholly because I am related to Adam. And I become a partaker in salvation for the one and only reason that I am a member of the race of which Christ is the representative.

Behold, here is *grace!*

All legacies are unmerited. I take over the fruit of that for which others have labored when I receive an inheritance. So also in things spiritual. There is nothing in me which causes me to merit salvation. I am saved simply because I belong to that race to which God gave a representative and substitute, who on my behalf made atonement to God for me and for all my sins.

This is what we mean when we say that *grace is free.*

It is for *all.* "God . . . would have all men to be saved, and come to the knowledge of the truth" (I Timothy 2:3-4). "He is the propitiation for our sins; and not for ours only, but also for the whole world" (I John 2:2). There is no distinction. All have sinned. But Christ has also made atonement for all. No sin is so small that it does not need to be atoned for. And no sin is so great that it cannot be atoned for. "The blood of Jesus his Son cleanseth us from all sin" (I John 1:7). There is only one sin that cannot be *forgiven,* that sin which we will not confess.

Grace is free.

By that we mean, further, that it can be received *gratis,* for nothing.

We are not to pay for it. "Ho, every one that thirsteth, come ye to the waters, and he that hath no money; come ye, buy, and eat; yea, come, buy wine and milk without money and without price" (Isaiah 55:1).

In non-figurative language this means: We are not to try to make ourselves deserving of being saved.

When God forgives us our sins, He does so entirely without any merit on our part, that is, there is in us no meritorious ground for it. Neither our conversion, our remorse, our prayers, our faith, or anything else in us can move God to love us and forgive us.

Nay, it is not by personal acquirement or merit, but by *inheritance* that salvation becomes ours. It is for no other reason whatsoever but that I have been born into a race to which God has given Christ, our Substitute, our Redeemer.

Grace is free.

This implies even more, yea, much more.

Not only that which we have already seen: that all may seek it. And receive it for nothing.

But this: that grace seeks us, goes after us, searches us out.

We say now and then that grace is as free *as air*. And this is a good expression. The air is, in the first place, free. We do not pay anything for it, while nearly all the other necessities of life cost something, more or less. We must even pay for water, at least most of us. But the air is free, at least yet. And there is enough of it. Everywhere. We do not need to make a journey to a neighboring community or city in order to get air.

Nor do we need to seek air. The air seeks us, surrounds us, wherever we are, and enters into our bodies, provided we do not in some way hinder it from doing so. How intrusive air is he knows best who has tried to produce a vacuum. In order to do this one must have very ingenious and delicate instruments. From our own experience we know that it is easier to breathe than to hold our breath, that is, keep the air out.

So it is with grace also.

God did not only reconcile the world unto Himself, II Corinthians 5:18-20; He also "gave us the ministry of reconciliation." He committed to His church the "word of reconciliation." "We are ambassadors therefore on behalf of Christ, be ye reconciled to God!"

Here we see how God deals with those who oppose Him and do not desire reconciliation. First He atones for our sins. Then He seeks us out one by one in order to bring us the news of the finished redemption, and thus transfer to us, to our own personal possession, that which according to the laws of heredity belongs to us, because we have been born into that race for which Christ has made atonement.

Through the means of grace, Word and Sacrament, God makes His way to each individual sinner. It is through these means that the inheritance seeks the heir.

+

That is why we were *baptized* as soon as we were born into this world.

We were at that time small indeed; we could neither speak, think, nor pray. Many believe that we for this reason should not baptize infants. They think that the little ones must grow up first, so as to be able to repent and believe before they are baptized.

But in doing so these people have forgotten two things:

First, that Jesus says: "Whosoever shall not receive the kingdom of God as a little child, he shall in no wise enter therein" (Mark 10:15). That is, people turn things around when they think that our little ones must become adults in order to become partakers in the gift of Baptism. It is, on the contrary, the adults who must "repent and *become as little children*" in order to enter into the kingdom of God. For God does not need any *help* in order to save us; He needs neither our prayers, our faith, our remorse, or anything else. All He needs is *access*. And that He has to little children. They can neither consciously nor wilfully hinder Him. Therefore God can without hindrance transfer the inheritance to these little "heirs." For the little ones are heirs, not only of original sin, but also of grace, because they are born into the race for which Christ has made atonement.

In the second place, these people have forgotten that the inheritance seeks the heir. They are still living in the delusion that the heir must make himself known and seek the inheritance. For that reason they think that a child should not be baptized until the child itself has become old enough to seek Baptism.

Here is a *fundamental misconception,* not only of Baptism, but also of the *grace* of God. These people have not gained an insight as yet into the most precious and most mysterious aspect of grace, namely, that it is not only free, but that it seeks out the sinner even before the sinner thinks of grace. It seeks him and presses in upon him, even enters into him, provided he does not do that which is the only thing a sinner can do in this connection, namely, deliberately and wilfully hinder God from transferring the inheritance to the sinner's personal possession.

The conversion, the penitence, and the faith of an adult are not something by means of which we *help* God to save us; they are much rather the deliberate choice whereby we, enlightened by the Spirit of God, determine *not* to hinder God from performing the miracle of salvation in our lives. Then is when we adults have become "as children," for the characteristic thing about the little child is nothing else but this: It does not hinder God from transferring the inheritance.

Why should the little child be baptized?

For no other reason than that it has been born into the race which was made sinful by Adam, but which has been redeemed by Christ. God has pledged Himself to transfer to every member of the race that atonement which belongs to the race because Christ was the representative of that race.

God meant this so literally that as soon as a human being is born He would have the inheritance seek out the child and become the child's personal possession. The *Word* as a means of grace cannot as yet be applied to the little one, because the use of the Word is predicated upon consciousness and will. But *Baptism* can be applied, because it penetrates with its divine effects deeper than to the consciousness and the will; it addresses itself to the unconscious depths of the soul. There sin and Satan are already at work. This is what we mean by the child's original or *inherited* sin. Now God, too, enters into the life of the little one and begins His work, alongside that of sin and Satan.

By physical birth the little child is made a partaker of Adam's life. By its new birth in Baptism the little one becomes a partaker of life in Christ. It is grafted as a little branch into the true vine, which is Christ. From now on it has life together with Christ.

That the little one lacks consciousness does not hinder a transmittal of life and a vital union such as this. As the little one shares in the life of its parents without doing anything to bring this about and without as yet being conscious thereof, so it also shares in the life of Christ, without as yet having any knowledge thereof and without having done anything to bring it about.

+

Behold, the inheritance has now found the heir.

The little child has received the whole inheritance, for it has through Baptism been united with Christ. God cannot give any one anything more than Christ, whether it be children or adults.

It is the same in the spiritual life as in the temporal. The little child *possesses* in Christ just as much while it is little as it will when it grows up. But it cannot as a child *make use of* the inheritance in the same way as when it has grown up and become of age.

Notice now how God continues to help the little one to appropriate unto itself the whole inheritance. As the child grows up and develops both consciousness and will, God seeks it by new means. It is true that the little one will also seek God, in prayer, in confession of sin, in repentance, in thanksgiving. But this is always a fruit of God's previous seeking of the child: through the Word, mediated by father, mother, brothers and sisters, servants, teachers, and pastors.

You fortunate reader, you who remained in the grace of your Baptism and never went out into the far country, what is it that you have experienced throughout the many years of your childhood, through the bitter and the sweet, through things that you could understand and things that you could not understand, what is it that you have experienced but this gracious intervention of God, which sought to accomplish only one thing: to help you *make use* of the gift of salvation which you received in Baptism?

As long as you were a child, you thought as a child, both about sin and about grace. Nor did God expect anything else of you. But at the time you began to "put away childish things," when you were "growing up" both physically and spiritually, then, too, God's grace pressed in upon you and entered into your life. And gave you an adult experience both of sin and of grace.

First you experienced struggles and sorrows, of a new kind, a kind hitherto unknown to you. You became utterly confused and bewildered. You thought perhaps that you had fallen away from God. But after a while you began to see that this was of God. He was helping you in this way to *see* and to *make use* of the fulness of that grace which you received when you were baptized. God permitted you to see your inherited sin in great measure: that you did not hate sin and did not love God as you ought, notwithstanding the beautiful and good life you had lived during your childhood and youth. As a result, the cross became your dearest place of refuge.

Notice again that it was the inheritance which sought you, and which became *yours* in the most personal sense of the term: yours, not only because God gave it to you in Baptism, but yours because you now as an independent and mature person made use of it.

+

But most people leave the Father-house and go on a journey into the far country as soon as they become old enough to decide in the matter. They do not wish to live their lives with Jesus looking on and with their conscience as their guide. They flee from the faith and the God of their childhood, and would prefer to avoid thinking any of life's serious thoughts. They despise the inheritance, and sell it, as Esau did, for a tasty dish of some kind.

However, they, too, experience, much to their surprise, that the inheritance pursues and seeks out the fleeing heir. Along all his crooked ways. Not only during his quiet hours, when the turmoil of the day has subsided. Not only during adversity, sorrow, and illness. Even in the midst of sinful joys and pleasures the inheritance would make itself known, and make sin bitter, distasteful, and uninviting.

Behold, here we are in touch with the *grace of spiritual awakening.*

We are awakened without our asking it, without our doing anything to be awakened. The only thing we do is to resist it and hinder it as long as we dare and as long as we are able to do so.

We are awakened from our sins simply and solely for Christ's sake, because we are members of the race of which Christ is the head. God has in mercy pledged Himself to transfer the inheritance to each individual member of this race, and not to give up this work, even though the sinner despises and flees from the legacy. God does not give up this work until the sinner has shut himself off forever, leaving God no way whatsoever of reaching his conscience with the divine call of the gospel. Not until then is such a person eternally lost.

God does not ask anyone for permission to awaken him from his sins.

This must not, however, be misunderstood. God does not compel people to become converted. Not at all. He will have no unwilling servants either in heaven or on earth. But He has in His unspeakable mercy reserved the right to stop every man upon his way in life and let none be eternally lost without first being awakened out of their sleep in sin and having their inheritance set before them, in order that they might freely decide whether to accept the inheritance and be saved, or turn away and enter into eternal darkness.

A person cannot, then, hinder God from awakening him.

In other words, the fact that we cannot help being awakened is a part of the inheritance, more particularly, that portion of the inheritance in which all men are permitted to share. Because man has been born into the race for which Jesus has made substitutionary atonement, therefore man is to have the inheritance offered to him and brought to him by God Himself. This is what God does when He awakens us.

+

But *awakening* is not the same as *conversion*.

There are many people who have been awakened but

who have not been converted. They could not avoid being awakened. God saw to that. But they are able to avoid being converted; because God does not *compel* any one to accept the inheritance. However, He does bring it to him and offer it to him.

Let us now see what conversion is and how it takes place. Never does *this* become clearer to us than when we see it in the light of our inheritance.

Conversion is misunderstood and misinterpreted in many ways, all due to the fact that men have not seen conversion in the light of God's grace, in the light of Christ's substitutionary atonement.

In one way or another men have looked upon conversion as something which man on his side must present to God before God can save him. Either in such a way that man by a decision of his own will must cut himself loose from his old sinful ways. Or in such a way that man by his own regret and sorrow must bring forth a new attitude of heart as the condition upon which God can forgive sin and make the sinner His child.

But to a sinner both of these ways are equally impossible. He is a *slave* of sin, John 8:34. And his slavery consists in this: his will wills to sin, even though he may fear the consequences of sin and therefore may seek to avoid those sins which are fraught with the greatest danger.

This view of conversion cannot be harmonized with the Bible's description of the human being as one who is completely lost in himself. If man could by his own will decide to give up his sinful life, and if man could by his own regret succeed in reaching a state wherein he hated sin, then verily he would not be saved by grace, but by good deeds.

Nay, conversion takes place in an entirely different manner.

By awakening him God has by a miracle brought the sinner face to face with Himself. In this heavenly light the sinner sees his sin in an entirely new light. First he sees his old sins, the small and the great. Then he sees his inner sins, his sinful imagination, his sins of thought and desire. Next he sees sin itself, the fact that he has the *will* to sin, and not that he does that which is sinful merely by accident. Finally, he sees that he cannot, in spite of his best efforts, change this sinful attitude of his.

Not until then is he ready for conversion.

And conversion is a choice. But the choice does *not* consist therein that he by a decision of his own will attempts to rid himself of his old sinful ways and by his regret seeks to reach a state in which he hates sin.

Nay, the choice concerns the *inheritance*.

Through his spiritual awakening the sinner has not only caught a glimpse of the inheritance, but he has begun to see also that he needs it. The only thing that he *can* and should decide now is this: *would* he accept the inheritance, or *would* he *not*.

In the Scriptures this is expressed in the following way: "Behold, I stand at the door and knock: if any man hear my voice and open the door, I will come in to him, and will sup with him, and he with me" (Revelation 3:20).

It is Jesus who knocks, and it is Jesus who enters in. The sinner can do only one of two things: either open or close his heart-door to Jesus when He knocks.

That which saves the sinner and transforms him from an unsaved to a saved person is therefore not *his* choosing, *his* prayers, *his* regrets, not even his faith. His salvation consists in this: that Jesus enters into his life with all His grace and His gift of salvation. But He must have the sinner's consent; for He will not force Himself upon any one.

Precisely as is the case with a death-sick patient. If he

is not operated upon at once, he will be death's certain prey. The operating surgeon is at hand; everything is in readiness for the operation. All that is necessary is the patient's consent. The latter is reluctant for a moment, but then asks the surgeon to proceed. And the patient is saved from death.

Was it his decision to permit himself to be operated that saved him? No, his decision did not affect his illness in the least.

Was it his request that the doctor proceed at once that did it? No, that could not bring about any improvement either.

Was it the pain or fear which accompanied his prayer that surgery be done? No, this would make him worse rather than better.

What was it then that wrought the change?

Simply this: that the patient by his decision *gave the surgeon permission* to perform the operation.

May I press the figure a little further: nor does recovery depend upon the *force* with which the patient gives his consent. He may be so weak that he can scarcely make his assent audible. Nevertheless, he will be rescued; all the doctor needs is a slight nod, indicating that he is to proceed with the operation.

Here, my awakened friend, you have the choice involved in conversion pictured to you very clearly.

As the patient himself cannot remove the illness from his body, so you, too, are unable to remove sin from your soul. But if you will give Jesus access to your soul, He will enter in and perform the operation.

Now notice that it is not the intensity of will with which you choose Christ, nor the passionateness or fervency of your prayer, nor the intensity of the pain with which you feel remorse which persuades Jesus to enter in and perform the saving operation in your life.

Nay, He does not do this for *your* sake but for *His* sake. He has not only atoned for your sins, once for all; He has also taken upon Himself the task of transferring the inheritance to every member of the race of which He is the representative. He *wills* to come in and He *comes* in to you with the inheritance in all its fulness as soon as you give up your resistance and give Him access.

You do not, therefore, by your conversion move Jesus to come and show mercy to you. It is Jesus who through your spiritual awakening moves you to repent, to open the door, that He might continue *within you* the good work which He up to this time has been doing *outside* your heart's door.

+

There are many who have made the choice involved in conversion. They have made a full accounting of everything to God and have brought everything into the light. They would not conceal or spare sin of any kind. It can be said of them in truth that they are walking *in the light.*

But many of them are still in great darkness and uncertainty. Without peace and without joy. And the reason for it all is this one thing: they cannot believe.

That is: they are happy and joyful and feel certain that they are children of God *now and then;* however, only very seldom. Doubt recurs with renewed strength. Everything becomes muddled and hazy, and they cannot attain to enduring assurance of sonship with God.

The worst of it is that they feel that there must be something radically wrong with them. They do not have the experience, of which they hear so much in sermons, that if they surrender themselves fully they will gain assurance, peace, and joy. No matter how much they surrender themselves, and no matter how much they search their hearts, they are as much in the dark as they ever were. Now and then, moreover, they become so deathly weary of it all that they scarcely know how to continue what seems to them to be a vain struggle indeed.

I think that we preachers are in a large measure responsible for this uncertainty. For some time now we have almost forgotten that God's salvation consists both in *killing* and in *making alive,* Deuteronomy 32:39; Romans 7:10-13. We have almost forgotten that God *kills* before He makes alive.

We are all by nature impatient. The people of our day are perhaps a little more impatient than has ordinarily been the case; we have become accustomed to speed in everything. Salvation, too, must take place rapidly. We have not time to wait for God to complete His *killing* work in our sinful hearts. We want to be made alive at once.

As a result we are as a rule very helpless in dealing with new converts who do not receive assurance and peace at once. Many deal harshly with them and tell them without further ado: if you would surrender yourself *completely* to the Lord, you would receive assurance. The fact that you do not have assurance shows that your surrender is not complete.

Others are not so harsh, but do not know how to deal properly with these people; these doubting souls do not fit into the scheme of things as they have formulated it. They really do not know what advice to give them.

This lack on the part of us who preach leads awakened souls into unnecessary struggles and needless suffering. They are compelled to suffer because of the shallow and superficial psychology and cure of souls employed by the present-day generation of Christian workers.

+

According to my knowledge of church history, our age seems to stand out as the only one which has made *this* mistake. Previous ages have on this point had a deeper insight into the soul-life of men, and have therefore been able to practice a more thorough-going cure of souls in dealing with these people than we have.

Augustine, Luther, Calvin, Arndt, Francke, Grundtvig, Hauge, Gisle Johnson are representative of diverse ages and church bodies. They had themselves experienced God's "killing" grace in a special way, and were therefore able also to understand and guide souls who were passing through conversion's "killing" period of storm and stress.

For this reason souls in days gone by were more advantageously orientated as far as these struggles were concerned. Obviously, they were not spared these struggles; for God must "kill" a sinner before He can make him alive. But they did enter upon these struggles with a much better *preparation* than awakened souls do these days.

They were taught beforehand by the preaching of their day that to surrender to God is not a mere pastime, that conversion is tantamount to losing one's life, the same as dying. They were also prepared in that they had been taught that this dying cannot take place without a *death-struggle*. They were also prepared in that they knew it might take some time before God had wrought completely that work in them which in the Scriptures is spoken of as "killing." They were taught moreover that this was a part of *salvation,* a part of God's saving *grace.* Above all, they learned to know that a previous generation of Christians had experienced this in connection with conversion. It was therefore easier for them to endure the pain and anxiety of this "killing." What they were suffering was not a sign that they had chosen a wrong way, but rather that they were in the hands of the right one, who "kills" before He makes alive.

In our day the spiritually awake are in a much more difficult position in this respect.

From us older Christians they undoubtedly get the impression that conversion not only can but also should bring them assurance at once. Preferably in such a way that one can stand up and testify immediately that one has gained assurance and peace.

And if they should go along for some time without joy and assurance, they begin to look upon their condition as an abnormal one, one bordering on morbidness. In sermons and in the cure of souls they seldom hear of other believers who have been in a similar condition. As a rule they are told of those to whom everything became clear at once.

As a result the struggles connected with conversion, with God's "killing" grace, are something which these seeking souls *cannot understand*. They are not prepared for such things. On the contrary, they have been led to believe that they will receive joy and assurance at once. When they do not, it is easy for them to think that they have been entirely mistaken.

+

That there are in our day so many such seeking souls, who have made a whole-hearted surrender to God but who have not as yet gained assurance, is not to me only an indication of weakness.

We are the children of an age which to an almost unbelievable degree had forgotten the *majesty of God*. We Christians, too, were guilty on this score. God had gradually become small and easy to understand. God and Christianity were as easy as kissing one's hand. Faith became a simple little piece of arithmetic: "Only believe and reckon, only believe and reckon!"

As a result we had many "believers" who knew little of the serious nature of sin and of fear of God. The gulf between God and sinners was about to disappear. They were not only unacquainted with the *fear and trembling* of which Paul speaks in Philippians 2:12; they even looked upon such things as slavery to the law.

Now God in His grace is helping us over into a new period. He has undermined the self-certainty and the ease with which our relationship to God has often been associated. We have begun to feel the gulf which there is between us and God.

The many souls in our day who are sincere but who are in a state of uncertainty are proof to me that God has once again been permitted to speak to us of *sin* in such a way that souls listen and understand. For the time being it seems that He must place the emphasis upon sin, in order that we might again realize the *need* of grace, and not only speak of it.

By this I do not by any means desire to imply that it is in and by itself a thing to be desired that awakened souls should not attain to assurance and peace. I have merely wanted to indicate that this is a feature of the physiognomy of our day which should not make us discouraged, but rather make us hopeful.

+

I take it for granted that there are among my readers many such seeking souls as I have here described. And now after having spoken *about* you, I am happy to have the opportunity of saying a word *to* you.

And it is, as you no doubt understand, about the *inheritance* that I would speak.

First, I shall speak briefly about faith; for you have misunderstood that somewhat. You think that you cannot believe, and you look upon that as the reason for your uncertainty and lack of peace. But it is in this that you are mistaken. You have faith, provided you confess your sins to God. It is stated very clearly in the Bible that

"If we confess our sins, he is faithful and righteous to forgive us our sins" (I John 1:9).

That is why the old Haugeans said: *To believe is to come to Christ with one's sins.* He who confesses his sins to God every day is a believer, whether he has assurance or not. For faith is not the same as assurance. Assurance is a form of faith, namely, its mature form. Faith is present before assurance, as the green blade is present before the mature corn in the ear.

This confusing of faith and assurance is an error which has caused seeking souls much bitter and unnecessary distress. Because they did not have assurance, they thought they did not have faith either. And since they thought they did not have faith, they thought also that they were unsaved.

Scripture brings full clarity into the situation. It says that *faith* is the *condition* upon which a sinner is saved; *assurance,* on the other hand, is a consequence, a *fruit* of salvation. Since Christ has died for our sins, all that is necessary on our part in order to be saved is to believe, and that means to come to Christ and confess our sins.

In the second place I shall point out the mistake which many make when they speak of *laying hold* of Christ by faith, or of *appropriating* to oneself the grace of God.

That this is one aspect of faith, we see from the Scriptures: Philippians 3:12, 13; I Timothy 6:12. But if we interpret the expressions "lay hold of" and "appropriate" in such a way that we make them mean that Christ cannot reach us unless we, as it were, lay hold of Him and draw Him down to ourselves, then we have completely misunderstood the words of the Scriptures. We have forgotten the most profound mystery in connection with grace, namely, that grace is not only for all and that it is free, but that it seeks out the sinner, even before the sinner thinks of grace. It seeks him and presses in upon him,

yea, enters into him, provided the sinner does not hinder
God from transferring the inheritance to his personal
possession.

Let us note the purpose of faith.

It is necessary: "without faith it is impossible to be
well-pleasing unto him" (Hebrews 11:6). But the purpose
of faith is not to draw the inheritance down to you. The
inheritance has already sought you, already knocked at
your heart's door. Your faith is the answer to God's
knocking, by which you open the door, by which you
cease your opposition to Him. And you cease opposing
God when you acknowledge all your sins before Him.

Our sincere confession of sin is that act of faith by
which we open our hearts to God. In the very instant
that we do so He enters in with the gift of grace in all
its fulness.

In the third place I shall mention a misunderstanding
that some people harbor. They think that they cannot
believe in the grace of God as long as they do not have
the joy and peace of assurance. This is a misunderstanding of *grace,* while the former was a misunderstanding of
*faith.*

The mistake occurs because people look upon grace in
a narrow and one-sided way as *life-giving grace* only, and
do not take into account *mortifying* grace.

This misunderstanding is deep-rooted.

That our age so frequently overlooks the mortifying
aspect of grace is due to our age's shallow sense of sin
and superficial view of human depravity.

The usual conversion-preaching of our day indicates
that we look upon the natural man as being ripe for conversion the moment he himself decides to be converted.
This shows a strange confidence in unregenerate humanity, and is not at all in agreement with the Bible's description of the natural man.

If conversion were nothing more than this, that the natural man, having been awakened and having begun to see that he is living an unregenerate life, now consciously and by the exercise of his will decides to repent, then verily conversion would not be the miracle which the Scriptures say it is. Nor would the will of the unregenerate man be as completely perverted as the Scriptures say it is.

Here we bring to light the superficiality of the current view of both sin and conversion. We think that an awakened person is ripe for God's *life-giving* grace the very moment that he decides to repent. By saying nothing to the contrary we acquiesce in the idea that that person's awakening has imparted to his unregenerate person a sufficient amount of God's *mortifying* grace. We think we are on the safe side when we emphasize as strongly as we can that from now on everything depends upon the *sincerity* of the awakened soul which is now making the choice involved in conversion.

But here we are most certainly mistaken.

Of course, sincerity is vital. But nevertheless it is not enough. A self-righteous person also may be subjectively sincere; that is, his actions may be in accordance with the light which he possesses.

Every Christian who is at all capable of self-observation will without any doubt acknowledge that he was by no means "killed" when he decided to yield to God. That which should and *must* be put to death, namely, the natural man's confidence in his own understanding and his own will, was as yet practically untouched. Our very decision, the choice which we made in conversion, was perhaps the best proof of the confidence we still had in the power of our own will. And therefore, too, we became alarmed when it appeared that the decision we had made with our own will did not bring the results we had expected.

And perhaps our wilfulness in connection with the decision we made to repent was even more unrestrained and unmitigated than we have indicated. From what we had read and heard we had perhaps made up our minds how things should take place when one is converted. But we experienced very soon that they did *not* take place in that way. Then we began, both consciously and unconsciously, to force ourselves ahead along the lines which we thought were the only right ones.

When we did not succeed in this either, then we became completely bewildered and disconsolate. But this confusion showed more clearly than anything else that we had not as yet given up our confidence in ourselves. We were certain that we had the *right* understanding of these things. Therefore we could not comprehend why everything did not go as we thought it should. It did not occur to us that we had an erroneous conception of the struggle involved in conversion and the course which it takes. For this reason it did not occur to us either that we should simply permit ourselves, like blind men, to be guided and led by Him who has known it all, even from eternity.

Naturally, the thing which seemed worst to us was that we did not attain to the *bliss* which we thought we had a right to expect when we had acted in such a commendable way as to really turn to God! Gradually the idea began to occur to us that it was strange of God, after all, not to give us what He had promised and what all believing Christians said we must get, and the sooner the better.

To begin with we scarcely dared to make room for such a thought. We felt that it was really not proper. But as time passed we became more and more impatient. We could not rid ourselves of the *thought,* even though it was not permitted to express itself in *words.*

During that period of stress and struggle many a strange thought coursed through our *rent* soul. Obstinate thoughts, defiant thoughts! Did we not even feel now and then that *we* were the injured party? Did we not feel as though we had some demands to make upon God? Demands that we be given assurance and peace? But God did not heed our demands. And that notwithstanding that we begged and prayed Him as imploringly as we knew how.

+

When an experienced Christian, later in his Christian life, begins to recognize these experiences from the time of his conversion, it becomes clear to him that the *mortifying* work of God's grace is not completed at the time of one's spiritual awakening, nor at the time that the decision to repent is made. He sees that it is *after* this decision has been made that God can in all seriousness begin to put to death our self-confidence and wilfulness.

Now some might ask: If the choice involved in conversion is not the decision to surrender oneself completely, to yield our own wills to God entirely, then what is it? Does this decision have *no* significance? Is it not, in that event, only a good resolution, one of many others, which an awakened person makes?

No, the decision involved in conversion retains its significance. It continues to be the decision which transforms a sinner from a *lost* to a *saved* sinner.

But it is true that this decision takes on a different meaning than the one ordinarily associated with it. The decision which the sinner makes obviously does not change anything in the sinner's will. That would be, like Münchhausen, to draw oneself up by one's own hair. The decision in itself means nothing as far as putting to death our

old ego. Therefore it means nothing whether the decision
is a strong one or a weak one.

That which does mean something, which imparts significance to the decision, is *that which* is decided; namely,
to yield myself into God's hands, to surrender myself to
Him to be dealt with by Him, to be given mortifying treat-
ment by Him if need be.

Just as with the patient we mentioned above. He is not
saved by his decision, regardless of how strong it may be.
His salvation, physically speaking, depends solely upon
*that which* he decides, namely, to let the surgeon operate.
It is the surgeon who brings about the change. And this
the surgeon does even though the decision of the patient
is very weak. All that is necessary is that the doctor be
given permission to proceed with the operation.

*The decision involved in conversion consists therefore
really in this, that the awakened sinner surrenders himself fully to the mortifying grace of God in order thereby
to be made alive in Christ.*

This is not easy for the sinner to see clearly at the time
of his conversion or during the struggles through which
he passes at this time. But were he given better guidance
by us preachers and older believers, his lot during these
struggles would be made easier in a number of respects.

In the first place, he would be *prepared* for the struggles and difficulties which are so characteristic of the time
of conversion. He would know that older Christians
experienced the same thing when they were converted.
It is true that this knowledge would not spare him this
suffering, but it would make it easier for him to hold out
during these pains of mortification.

The *unintelligibility* of it all would be removed.

We know from our experience with physical ailment
that it is much easier to endure pain when our doctor
understands what is wrong with us and can tell us that

this is the way this sickness always acts, and that it is not dangerous even though it is painful.

In the second place, if this were done it would be easier for the newly converted to look upon these painful inner experiences as the *work of God.*

The way new converts ordinarily look upon these things now is that these painful experiences are not at all the work of *God,* but, on the contrary, a result of the sinner's own activity, by which he is continually *disturbing* the work of God in his soul.

Could he, on the other hand, see that the impotence, anxiety, and despair which he experiences during this time are a fruit of God's mortifying work, then he would see that it is a part of God's *grace.*

As a result of the instruction that awakened souls are ordinarily given these days, many of them look upon these experiences as the clearest proof that they have as yet not been made partakers of the grace of God. For by grace they understand only *life-giving* grace, above all assurance and peace.

In the third place, if the newly converted were given the proper guidance it would be easier for them to "humble themselves under the mighty hand of God," and not be as impatient as they are in *demanding* assurance and joy.

Their *longing* for assurance would be the same, and this longing is a sound and normal thing. But if they could see that they already have the grace of God, that grace has sought them out and found them, yea, even penetrated into their being from the very moment that they confessed their sins, then it would be easier for them to reconcile themselves to God's mortifying dealings with them.

Then, too, they would learn more quickly to "believe without seeing." It would be easier for them to learn that which God during this difficult period is trying to teach

them, namely, to believe the *Word,* without *feeling* the
workings of God's grace.

In the fourth place, they would in this way be able to
see more clearly that it is not they themselves who are to
force assurance out of their wretched, doubting, uncertain
souls; but that assurance is a fruit of the continuing work
of the Lord, which consists in transferring the inheritance
to the sinner's personal possession and personal use. And
as God freely and without being asked to do so wrought
spiritual awakening, repentance, and faith, so will He also
work assurance. Moreover, He does not *delay,* even
though it may take some time. He always does it as
quickly as He can. For assurance, too, is a part of the
inheritance. And the inheritance must needs be transferred to the individual sinner, because each one is a member of the race whose representative and substitute Jesus
is.

+

Before I bring this portion to a close, may I say a few
words about the *responsibility* which the inheritance places
upon the sinner. To me this responsibility never stands
out more clearly than when I look at it from the viewpoint which we have just considered.

Many people think that they are not converted for the
simple reason that they are not able to convert themselves.

They *would,* but they *cannot.*

Why they cannot do it, perhaps is not clear to them.
But that they cannot, of this they are certain.

Should this book fall into the hands of any one who
thinks thus, then let me say at once: you are completely
mistaken.

I feel a desire to say even more: Be careful that you
are not *dishonest* with yourself here. Do you yourself
believe what you are saying? Is there not a voice within
you which says: "It is only an *excuse* which you are mak-

ing in order the more easily to get rid of the idea of conversion. You could have been saved if you had only wanted to!"

One thing in particular God provided for when He established His covenant with the human race: to bring the inheritance very close to every member of the race. Yes, even more: to bring it into the very heart of every human being, provided they did not deny Him access thereto.

He has come to you with the inheritance.

You did not bid Him come, but He came nevertheless. He gave you the grace of awakening. He spoke to you of His love, until sin became acrid and bitter to you.

*Then* He asked you, *"Would* you be made whole?"

When you answered, "I cannot," then you did not answer the question that He was asking you. He did not ask you if you *could* heal yourself, but if you *would* that He should make you whole.

Let us turn back again to the patient I mentioned before.

Imagine now that the operating surgeon stands in readiness. He has just explained to the patient what his condition is, told him that an operation will save his life, and that he is now ready to begin the operation. The doctor says finally, "Is it your will that we proceed?"

Suppose the patient said, "Yes, I am very willing, but I cannot!" You would think, would you not, that he was not in his right mind. For the doctor did not ask if the dying man could operate on himself, but if he wanted to be operated upon by the doctor.

The Physician of Souls stands at your side. Your soul is sick unto death.

He does not ask you if you *can* cease being a worldling, but if you would have Him make a new man of you.

He does not ask you if you *can* refrain from your old bosom sins, but if you would have Him loose the chains that bind you to sin.

He does not ask you if you *can* begin to hate sin and to love God, but if you would have Him create within you this new attitude of heart and mind.

He does not ask if you *can* make yourself feel at home with God and gladly do His will, but if you would that He should give you this new nature, which is in its element when it is with God.

He does not ask if you *can* gladly give up that worldly joy and desire which has hitherto been your life, but if you would that He should give you a joy and desire which would cause you willingly and gratefully to give up that joy which cannot endure the presence of God.

Behold, *this* is your responsibility, my awakened friend!

He asks you only what you *would* do, what your *will* is. You recognize too, perhaps, that this is the reason for your great anxiety during the period of your awakening. You are uncomfortably conscious of the fact that the decision which your awakening compels you to make is the very decision which will make manifest what your will is.

What your very innermost will is.

Either: remain sick at heart and continue to rule your own life in a selfish way.

Or: surrender your wilfulness, permit the Great Surgeon to operate, and—be made whole!

# A Contrite Heart

*"I dwell in the high and holy place, with him also that is of a contrite and humble spirit, to revive the spirit of the humble, and to revive the heart of the contrite."*　　　　　　　　　　　　Isaiah 57:15

MEN fill the world with their sins. Sins of every kind and of every degree.

Conscious sin and unconscious sin. Individual sin and social sin. National sin and international sin.

Open sin and secret sin. Sin that is afraid, and which conceals itself in dark places. And bold sin, openly committed.

Oh, how men sin in this world of ours!

What must not God look upon, night and day! That He can endure us human beings! He is past finding out, also when we consider this aspect of His being.

But the worst thing about man is not that he *does* that which is sinful.

The *heart* of man, which he carries in his bosom, is worse than all the sin he does.

"For from within, out of the heart of man, evil thoughts proceed, fornications, thefts, murders, adulteries, covetings, wickedness, deceit, lasciviousness, an evil eye, railing, pride, foolishness,"—Mark 7:21-22.

Jesus has here pointed out to us the ever-flowing source of sin, from whence it makes its way to all the earth, turning this earth into a fore-court of hell itself.

And still,—the worst thing about the heart is not that it is full of sin.

The worst thing about it is its *hardness,* its enmity and rebelliousness toward God. It *is* hard by nature. And it *makes itself* even harder toward God.

+

Most people live their life *far away* from God.

In our country, as in most countries that have been Christianized, a disagreeably large percentage of people practically never hear the Word of God. And it is to be feared that those who do not hear the Word scarcely ever read it at home either. Nor is it likely that they pray.

This is not good. In fact, it is so bad that it makes us feel quite helpless in the face of the godlessness of it all.

But the worst thing about these people is not that they are far away from God. The worst is that they *want to live that way.* They desire to avoid God and His Word.

Then there are others who *seek* God.

They go to church, perhaps every Sunday. Many participate in the Lord's Supper also. They read the Bible, too; perhaps every day. And pray a brief prayer, perhaps the Lord's Prayer.

But their *heart* is hard.

They do not *seek* God to *find* Him. On the contrary, they make use of worship as a means of avoiding a personal meeting with the living God.

They appoint themselves to sonship with God, and give themselves the forgiveness of sins. But they will not turn to God. If they on occasion hear a message concerning repentance, they become highly irritated. And *harden* their hearts against the God of grace.

Then there are some who recognize that they must repent.

They submit to the Biblical truth that "except ye turn, and become as little children, ye shall in no wise enter into the kingdom of heaven" (Matthew 18:2). Moreover, they acknowledge that they are not converted.

But when the call to conversion comes to them, then, too, they harden their hearts: they *postpone* their conversion. They say that they want to be converted, but not now. This, too, is a lie. For if a person really desires to be converted, then he must do it now, and not later. If a man is drowning in a lake he will not say: "I want to be saved, but not now!"

Finally, there are some who recognize that to postpone conversion is out of the question. But notice how we encounter the hardness and rebelliousness of the human heart also here.

There are many who want to be converted, but at the least possible cost. They try to bargain with God. They want *peace,* because their present state is so miserable. But they do not desire to make an *accounting* before God. There is some little sin, some sinful relationship or other, which they will not give up. So they continue to bargain with God, hoping to persuade Him to give them peace without a complete break with sin and without an honest accounting before Him.

Others will agree to a reconciliation, and they do not think of smuggling sin of any kind into their relationship with God. But notice how hard, rebellious, and unwilling their heart is. They want to be Christians *in secret!*

Listen also to the good reasons they are able to give when the Lord speaks to them about confessing His name before men and not being ashamed of Him.

They say: one's relationship to God is the finest and most intimate thing in a person's life. And if one begins to talk about these things, the result will be profanation, desecration. One would only lose the whole thing. No, one should only speak to God about these things, says the obstinate heart.

And if they feel that this is in direct conflict with our Lord's own words, Mark 8:38, then the rebellious heart says: "What shall I confess? I must at least be permitted to wait before I say anything until my life has made it manifest that I really have had a change of heart!"

Verily, the heart of man is hard.

+

No one can become a Christian without having his hard heart made *contrite*.

And it is *God* who makes hearts contrite.

But this is a difficult task, even for God.

When He created the universe with its countless solar systems, He sat calmly upon His royal throne in heaven, merely speaking the creative word. And in ruling this whole multitudinous creation, from the greatest planets and down to the smallest bacilli, He also sits quietly in His heaven, "upholding all things by the word of his power," Hebrews 1:3.

But when He was to make contrite the little but hard heart of man, then He could not remain seated on His royal throne. He had to leave His heavenly abode, come down to our earth, become a man, suffer, and die to atone for our sins.

To such great lengths did the Almighty have to go in order to make contrite the heart of man!

It is indeed a mighty miracle of God. The longer I live and the more I study this miracle, the greater it becomes to me. I am not certain whether a greater miracle ever takes place *within us* than when God makes contrite our heart of stone. There is perhaps only one miracle that is greater than this, and that is God's own incarnation.

*How* God does it, I cannot say.

This is the mystery in connection with spiritual awakening, its miraculous aspect.

And though I by the grace of God experienced this miracle twenty-seven years ago, I cannot to this day say how God did it. The only thing about which I can express myself is the *effect* of the miracle which I experienced in my soul.

Even the *time* at which our spiritual awakening occurs may be exceedingly enigmatic.

Most people live long periods of their life thoughtlessly and comparatively untouched by the call of God unto repentance. The remarkable thing is that these people are not heedless of the call of God only in days of prosperity and when the course of their life is smooth and calm On the contrary, many live through serious illnesses, sorrow, and many other adversities without becoming contrite of heart. They only become harder, and it becomes more and more difficult for God to gain access to their lives.

But then the miracle takes place, suddenly or more or less gradually. Often when no one was expecting that they would have a change of heart.

Nor was it any less unexpected to these people themselves.

They had not prayed that they might be awakened. They had neither willed nor desired nor thought of it. Therefore it came to them, not only as a surprise, but also at a very inconvenient time. This is also one of the reasons why so many who have been awakened spiritually *postpone* their conversion.

We *believe* that God works on a sinner's heart at all times, also when the sinner is living a life of thoughtlessness and levity. Therefore we believe also that God has been making preparations for this brief period of awakening for a long time in the life of the sinner, without his being aware of it, and that He has made these preparations very thoroughly.

But this, too, is enigmatic and mysterious.

And this, too, shows us how *difficult* it is even for God to bring about the spiritual awakening of a soul, to make

the heart of man contrite. The times that God can get
our attention and really speak to us are really few and
very brief. He must use the rest of the time in preparation
for these brief but decisive moments, when the call of God
reaches into our conscience and our will.

It is for this reason that the prophet cries out: "Seek
ye the Lord while he may be found; call ye upon him
while he is near!"—Isaiah 55:6.

The time in which the Lord may be found is the time
of spiritual *awakening*. The miracle in connection with
spiritual awakening is this: the Lord is *near*.

Why is not the Lord always near the sinner? Is it
because He does not care equally much for the sinner at
all times? We need only to ask and the answer is at hand:
the Lord is *unchangeable* in His love and care. The reason that He is not equally near the sinner at all times is
because it is not possible for Him.

The Lord must spend a great deal of time and use many
means in preparing the few moments in a sinner's life
when He will be able to get so near to the sinner that the
sinner will be compelled to hear God's call.

It is for this reason that the unconverted commit their
greatest sins when a spiritual awakening is in progress.
If at such a time they harden their hearts against the holy
conviction which has been imparted to them, then the
season of spiritual awakening witnesses a greater harden-
ing of heart than any other period in a sinner's life.

It is for this reason that the exhortation comes to us so
fervently: "Today if ye shall hear his voice, harden not
your hearts"—(Hebrews 3:15).

+

The brief season of spiritual awakening is, then, the
time that the Lord is near.

This in turn means: the nearness of the Lord is the
*miraculous* element in connection with our awakening.

In that moment, which the Lord has been such a long time and so diligently preparing, He suddenly compels the sinner to stand in His presence. In *that* moment the sinner cannot avoid standing before God.

This is the unspeakably gracious aspect of our spiritual awakening, that God does not permit a sinner to enter into eternal torment without first having met God face to face. Thereby God has compelled the sinner to face the truth, to come to himself, and decide whether he will per- mit himself to be saved or he will continue upon his hap- less way to perdition.

Now the sinner must decide.

He may choose whatever course he will. But choose he must, one of two things: either to *remain* in the near- ness of God or to flee from it. Without his choosing he has entered into this holy nearness to God into which his awakening has brought him. But now he must himself decide whether to remain therein or not.

Most people refuse to live their lives in God's nearness. Consequently they close their heart's doors at once. They can do that. By their own wills they can sever the con- nection with God which was brought about, without con- sulting their will, by their awakening.

But there are some who cannot endure to make their heart that hard. Really they also decide not to remain in the presence of God. What saves them is this, that they do not break off entirely the connection with God which has been established as a result of their awakening.

These awakened souls continue to live in the divine presence into which they have been brought as a result of their awakening. And *this* becomes their salvation. For God is so divine that the sinner needs only *experience* God, live in the nearness of God, in order to be made con- trite of heart.

This may take place very quickly, but as a rule it takes time. And takes place by degrees.

In the nearness of God we are *alone*.

Even though we sit in a large audience, we lose sight of men. We can no longer hide from God in a crowd. It is *I* to whom God speaks.

In God's nearness we all become *small*.

We feel the great gulf between us and God. And we feel that God has absolute authority over us. Here one speaks to me to whom I must listen, and with whom I cannot debate or compromise myself. It is only for me to listen and to give heed.

In the nearness of God we all become conscious of our *sinfulness.*

Our awakening brings us into a heavenly super-light, which to begin with seems quite unendurable. Our past sins array themselves against us. Little sins and great sins. Sins that we long since had forgotten emerge into our conscious mind and cause us much distress and pain.

Nor does the light only cast its rays backwards, upon our past; its rays are also directed inwardly. We become aware of our *inner* sinfulness. And that which we see is so horrible that we do not know where to turn our eyes. We behold a bottomless and boundless ocean of uncleanness and filth: self-love, pride, love of display, falsehood, envy, bitterness, hatred, sensuality, and lasciviousness.

In God's nearness we are also permitted to *see God*.

When we do, we see something the like of which we have never dreamed. Like all the sons of Adam we have a caricature of God in our minds. We think that He is strange and one with whom it is difficult to have any dealings, that He is so hard and brutal that He almost rejoices when He can cast a person into hell for not promptly submitting to His strict will and allowing himself to be saved into His heaven.

Then we meet God! The real God! We are permitted to see God as He comes to us in Christ. As a result, all our erroneous conceptions give way, one by one. He is no gruesome tyrant, but my best friend. He allowed Himself to be tortured to death in order to help such as I.

And now He stands at my side, not as my stern judge, with reproaches and harsh words, as I had thought. Nay; He looks upon me with eyes of compassionate and friendly love, and observes how wretched is my condition and how bad I feel.

He speaks to me. And it is remarkable how easy it is to understand what He says: "You are miserable. There is no one else who can help you now. Give me an opportunity, and I shall save you from the great misfortune of your life, your sin and your guilt."

But we are unable to make up our minds. We hesitate and really do not know what we want to do. At least, we do not accept His outstretched hand. Then we see that this hand is pierced. And we see also that He weeps for us.

*Then* is when it is hard to sin. *Then* is when sin becomes acrid and bitter. Before, sin was great fun; now it is a most gruesome reality. And our conscience pains us every time we perpetrate our customary sins.

Then we say to ourselves: this is all! We begin an energetic struggle against our sins. And we feel fairly certain that nothing more is needed. Now there can no longer be any question; we are determined to become new creatures and live new lives.

The greater becomes our disappointment therefore when we discover that we fail in this our resolve. We condemn and despise ourselves after our failures. And we make new resolutions, stronger than the preceding. But we fail again as badly as ever.

To begin with it is easy to excuse ourselves somewhat.

We blame our failures chiefly to our unfavorable environment and our old associates. But as time passes we are compelled to face the fact that the reason for our defeats is simply this: we carry within ourselves a desire toward sin which is stronger than our good resolutions.

This desire toward sin need only encounter the hell-fire of temptation. Then it rises at once to the boiling point, and all our good resolutions disappear, leaving no trace of themselves.

Verily, nothing is more humiliating to an awakened soul than this *struggle*. He had never before known that he was such a wretch, one who drifted spinelessly along with the stream, the hideous and dangerous stream of sinful desire.

But he experiences even greater things in the nearness of God.

In his distress this awakened soul has long since turned to God. But he found that this, too, was difficult. Formerly he had been of the opinion that it was a simple and easy matter to turn to God, after he had once decided to repent. Now he finds that it is unspeakably difficult. His courage fails him.

He knows very well that God is gracious and accepts sinners. But he reasons that these sinners must, of course, be repentant sinners, such as have declared that they will have nothing more to do with their former sins and who come to God with sincerely repentant hearts. He is not such a soul, he feels. The question that torments him constantly is this: can he turn to God at all, as long as he has not as yet succeeded in overcoming his old sins?

The first thing to which he now looks for consolation is his *grief* at having sinned.

He feels that it is natural that God is angry with him on account of his sins. But when God sees how he grieves because of his condition, will He not then have compassion on him and receive him nevertheless?

And the more anxious his perturbed soul becomes on account of his sinfulness the more hope he thinks he has of receiving grace from God. Thus he struggles on between fear and hope during the early period of his awakening.

Meanwhile he finds that these immediate and strong feelings gradually diminish in intensity. Our soul-life is so constituted that it cannot move very long at a time on the heights of such strong emotions as these. The thoughts which to begin with made such a profound impression on our emotional life, gradually become familiar and commonplace. The sinner continues to see his sinfulness and its dangerous consequences, but it no longer affects his feelings as it did formerly.

Then this awakened soul really becomes restless.

He feels that he can no longer even repent of his sins. His heart is as cold as ice and as hard as stone. The Bible speaks of people whom the Spirit has forsaken. Now he asks himself: I wonder if I am one of those whom the Spirit of God has given up because He saw that it was utterly impossible to do anything with me?

+

Behold, the sinner's heart has been made contrite!

God has performed a miracle. The sinner's mouth has been stopped and he has become guilty before God. Now he has no more *excuses* to offer, no *objections* to make to what God says to him.

Now he does not seek to bargain with God any longer about retaining some sin or other. But engages in a life and death struggle with all his sins. And it is his anguish and sorrow, yea, his despair, that he cannot rid himself of all of them.

Now he would hide sin no longer. He would make a complete accounting. His great fear now is that there might be guile in his spirit. Therefore he would gladly turn his heart inside out, if this were possible, in order to be absolutely certain that there was nothing there that had not been included in the accounting.

Now he does not seek to argue himself out of bearing the reproach of Christ any longer.

He assumes this reproach gladly, and willingly exposes himself to the thickest fusillades of enemy fire. Now his fellow-men may smile and laugh, yea, scoff and jeer, all they wish. He is determined to share His Saviour's reproach.

Now he *surrenders* to God.

Without naming any conditions or requirements. The great thing, yea, the exceedingly great thing, to him now is that God can and will accept him. By a mighty miracle of God he has become a helpless sinner, who never feels as secure at any time as when he is at the foot of the cross.

"I dwell in the high and holy place, with him also that is of a contrite and humble spirit, to revive the spirit of the humble, and to revive the heart of the contrite" (Isaiah 57:15).

Here God tells us where He dwells.

Do not all people know that? Oh yes, in a way. But not really. Therefore it is necessary to learn this from God Himself.

"I dwell in the *high place*."

It is important that we remember this when we turn to God in prayer. It was for this reason also that Jesus would have us begin our prayers with this thought: "Our Father, who art in *heaven*."

Our prayer life, yea, our whole life on earth, would be entirely different if we would keep clearly before our minds the fact that God dwells *in heaven*.

But then God tells us in the same breath that He also has another dwelling place: "with him also that is of a humble and contrite spirit."

He *dwells* there, He says.

The place where we dwell we call our home. God tells us here, therefore, that He *feels at home* in a contrite heart. Such a heart is dear and precious to God.

It is undoubtedly such hearts Jesus has in mind when He in the beginning of the Sermon on the Mount says: "Blessed are the poor in spirit: for theirs is the kingdom of heaven. Blessed are they that mourn: for they shall be comforted. . . . Blessed are they that hunger and thirst after righteousness: for they shall be filled" (Matthew 5:3-6).

Many a child of God reads these words with a deep sigh.

Before, these words were to them almost the most precious ones in the whole Bible. That was when they knew nothing else but hunger, thirst, sorrow, and poverty. How these words at that time opened wide the door of grace to their wretched souls! What gentle and healing balm were they not to the smarting wounds of conscience! They afforded encouragement, even though we had nothing else to lay before God but defeat.

But now these words do not have the same meaning to these children of God.

They have become threatening words of judgment. When the heart does not hunger and thirst after righteousness, but after all sorts of temporal things, of what benefit then is God's goodness and mercy? Has not He Himself also passed judgment upon them: "But woe unto you, ye that are full now! For ye shall hunger. Woe unto you, ye that are rich! For ye have received your consolation" (Luke 6:24-25).

When the heart does not grieve, but is cold and hard and indifferent, of what benefit then is Jesus in all His atonement? Even though Jesus were dead twice for sinners, He cannot forgive those who do not even mourn over their sins.

And when there is no longer any poverty of spirit, but the heart is satisfied and full of all manner of other things, leaving no room for or need of the good things of the kingdom of God, of what benefit is it then that grace is free?—Thus they reason!

At such times it is not easy to be a child of God. Nor is it easy to read these words of Jesus from the Sermon on the Mount.

One feels completely isolated from both God and His friends. When one sees and hears other Christians deriving consolation and satisfaction from the Word of God, one feels doubly condemned. One feels as though he is frozen in by the coldness of his own heart. Everything we resort to seems to turn cold, simply because we touch it. It seems to us that even other Christians become cool when we come near them.

Listen now, my friend, to what *God* says!

He dwells in your contrite heart. He feels at home there.

"No, not with me! My heart is no longer contrite," you say.

There, fortunately, you are mistaken. You misunderstand what is meant by a contrite heart. You do not know what it looks like on the inside.

If you would take a glass tumbler and throw it with all your might to the floor, then you would see what a glass tumbler looks like that has been completely broken. It lies there in a thousand pieces. And there is no expert who can put it together again.

Which is exactly what takes place with the human heart when God breaks it, makes it contrite. It lies there, completely broken to pieces. There is nothing whole about it ; nor can any one mend it. Faith and love, remorse and sorrow, prayer and reading of the Bible, sacrifice and self-denial,—all have been broken to pieces. You sit looking at the particles. And to you everything seems utterly hopeless. But you forget that it is God who has broken your heart. In order to find a place there. In order to dwell there. In order to feel at home there again.

The same thing had happened to you as happened to all the rest of us. After you had received life in God and had been received into intimate fellowship with God, you began little by little to rejoice more in the fruits of grace than in grace itself. When you lived in the felt grace of God, which you experienced after you had been set free, then it was really fairly easy for you to be a Christian. Without realizing it, you began to trust more in your Christianity than in Christ. A certain obviousness and self-complacency began to characterize your relationship to God. You had such an abundance of faith that you almost felt as though you could share some of it with others. Holy fear and trembling had almost disappeared from your life during all this spiritual prosperity.

Then God had to save you.

And therefore He made you broken-hearted a second time.

And how easily He did it ! He simply hid His face from you for a moment.

"A little while, and ye behold me not." "Ye shall weep and lament, but the world shall rejoice : ye shall be sorrowful, but your sorrow shall be turned into joy." "I will see you again, and your heart shall rejoice, and your joy no one taketh away from you."—John 16 :19-22.

He did not take His grace from you, only His *felt* grace.

And there you were, left with a heart which was empty, distant from God, unspiritual, cold, worldly, and hard. But then you had again become one of the poor in spirit.

For he is poor who does not have the most necessary things. And you, well, you had nothing. You had been stripped of everything.

But now there was room for God again in your heart. Now He felt at home with you again. For now you had nothing to cling to but Him. Now you did not have so many or such great things to say about it all. All the great things about yourself had been shattered to pieces. It was a joy to Jesus to see your supplicatory glances, which without great words or demonstration of any kind clung to His wounds and stripes. He saw now how you quietly and humbly found your place at the foot of the cross. He saw now your contrite heart's complete dependence upon Him "who was made unto us wisdom from God, and righteousness and sanctification, and redemption."

Why does God feel at home in your broken and contrite heart?

Because only the contrite heart can honor and worship the cross and the Crucified One. Only a contrite heart can admit that God is right in the crushing judgment which His cross passes upon the race as a whole and upon the individual. And only a contrite heart can acknowledge that God has the right to impart the unfathomable grace of the cross, and let the grace of God be what it is and reveal itself in all its fulness.

My broken-hearted and contrite friend! We cannot honor God more than by believing His grace. It is for this reason that He makes us contrite of heart.

# Religion and Christianity

THE relationship between Christianity and the religions of the world has engaged the thinkers of the human race from the beginning of Christianity down to our day.

In the early period of the church it was the *apologists* who took up this work. In the Middle Ages it was the *scholastics,* whose thinking circled about this problem continually. But on account of their unevangelical view of Christianity, especially in regard to sin and grace, the thinking of the scholastics led to a most grandiose admixture of Christianity and paganism.

*Luther* brought clarity also into this situation by his Biblical view both of man's sin and of God's justifying and new-creating grace. Both in his theology and in his preaching he never tires of showing the fundamental difference between the natural man's self-chosen, strained religiosity on the one hand and the free and happy relationship to God of the regenerate soul on the other.

The later *Lutheran theologians* continued the work, in harmony with the fundamental viewpoints of the Reformation. And sought to strengthen the Lutheran position with the idea of two kinds of revelation, the natural, upon which all pagan religiosity is based, and the supernatural, upon which Christianity rests.

But also on the Protestant side we find a movement which definitely seeks to obliterate the distinction between Christianity and paganism, to practice syncretism on a large scale. We notice this movement as early as the century of the Reformation. First in Italy and Switzerland, under the influence of the *Renaissance,* that is, the revived form of ancient paganism. From these circles came the *Socinians* and other rationalistic sects.

These groups continued, though rather quietly and unnoticed, their attempts to effect both a theoretical and practical blending of religions for some time. By the beginning of the eighteenth century these ideas had had an opportunity to develop, with the result that they spread throughout the domains of practically all the Protestant churches.

In church history this movement is known as *rationalism,* which name is significant enough, even though it does not tell us that rationalism is the Protestant parallel to the syncretism of Catholicism.

Energetic attempts have been made to build defenses against this modern syncretistic movement. Particularly after the great awakenings around the year 1800 were these efforts successful in most of the Protestant communions. But from 1850 and down to our day syncretism has flourished more than ever.

The most recent scientific discipline, comparative religion, has put not a little wind into the sails of the movement. The *history of religion,* the *psychology of religion,* and the *philosophy of religion* have all, following the well known scientific principle of analogy, sought to bring Christianity down to the same level as religion in general, in all essentials. There is disagreement, it is true, among the scholars concerning many of the details, but they are in perfect accord with reference to one thing: there is no *fundamental* difference between Christianity and other religions.

It is true that most of them prefer Christianity to the other religions. But this is not because they look upon Christianity as the only religion by which a man can be *saved.* Not at all; they think that every one will be saved by whatever faith he has. They do think, however, that

Christianity is the religion which offers man the most help and imparts to him the greatest amount of spiritual wealth.

Of late this blending of religions has been stimulated by the noticeable *religious unrest* which prevails throughout the entire civilized world. Modern man is realistic enough to see that religion is an organic and therefore an indispensable part of the life of the human spirit. He feels empty and weary, as people do who for some time have been compelled to do without proper nourishment.

Modern man wants religion.

And what modern man wants, is dished up to him without interruption.

The *newspapers* are quick to write about religion. Not only do they publish Sunday meditations,—which is almost the most tiresome form of religion to many. They also discuss religion. And since the newspapers look upon it as their special duty to bring the public the *latest news,* they naturally give special prominence to the latest and newest forms of religion that make their appearance. Every new discovery and improvement also in the field of religion is given much space and set in heavy type.

Our *authors* also write on religious subjects for the benefit of modern man.

I wonder if a single book of *belles-lettres* is published these days that does not contain a little religion. In every other field of life some knowledge of the subject upon which one writes is required, but this is not considered necessary in the field of religion. There everybody is an authority. So they continue to write, and to tell modern man what to do when he desires to be religious. And since Christianity ranks highest on the religious stock exchange, they refer without further ado to the religion they are teaching as Christianity.

The tragedy of the religious unrest of our age is that

modern man is so ignorant of what real Christianity is that he permits himself to be fooled into accepting almost any kind of imitation and falsification of true Christianity.

In this regard the upper classes seem to be in a worse situation than the lower. The ignorance of the former as far as religion is concerned is in shrieking contrast to the culture and the education of which they are so proud. They have forgotten their childhood instruction in the truths of Christianity, if they have ever had any such instruction. And they do not read the Bible.

When religious unrest comes, they become a comparatively easy and certain prey of some modern mixer of religions, whether a clergyman or not.

+

What does Christianity itself say about its relationship to the other religions?

We turn to the Scriptures.

Here we see even in the Old Testament that the *mixing of religions* was the great and persistent temptation which confronted the chosen people. That is why their first commandment read: "Thou shalt have no other gods before Me" (Exodus 20:3).

We can not express more clearly than this the relationship between the religion of Israel and the heathen religions: It was *sin* for the Israelites to participate in heathen worship ceremonies. It was, in fact, the worst sin they could commit, according to the testimony of both the law and the prophets.

Turning to the New Testament, we see that syncretism, or the mixing of religions, was a temptation also to the early Christians. Thus in Corinth. There were some who thought that it was perfectly proper for them to participate with their pagan relatives in the social fellowships connected with the sacrificial meals. This, they opined, was not in the least dangerous, since they did not participate in the pagan sacrifices themselves. Added to this was the fact that they with their keen intellects had discerned the fact that there are no idols in reality. Therefore, according to their way of thinking, a sacrificial meal was nothing else but simply and purely another meal.

It is in connection with this that the apostle gives the admonition and warning contained in I Corinthians 10.

Here he says that it is true that there are no idols. For there is only one God. But, he says further, this must not be taken to mean that the worship of the heathen is for this reason a worship of the one true God. Not at all. "The things which the Gentiles sacrifice, they sacrifice to demons, and not to God" (10:20). And he says expressly that they by their sacrifices "have communion with demons," "partake of the table of demons" (10:20-21).

Hence the admonition, "Neither be ye idolaters" (10:7), "flee from idolatry" (10:14—cfr. II Corinthians 6:14-18). And in Galatians 5:20-21 the apostle lists idolatry together with *adultery* and *murder*.

The apostle's view of the pagan religions does not, meanwhile, hinder him from seeing their divine purpose and plan. Their purpose is indicated in Acts 17:27: "that they should seek after God." He says further that God "left not himself without witness" unto the Gentiles (Acts 14:17), but in *history* (Acts 17:26; 14:17), in *creation* (Romans 1:19-20), in their *consciousness of the divine* (Romans 1:28), and in their *conscience* (Romans 2:14-15) revealed to them His existence, His nature, and His prerogatives.

The apostle here gives expression to the fact that it is in accordance with God's plan of creation and with the nature of man that the heathen are religious and that they have their worship-ceremonies.

But this does not in any wise alter his judgment with respect to their religiosity and worship itself. It is sinful, he says, and is related to demons, not to God. In Romans 1:18-32 he shows *why* the pagan religions are sinful. The heathen have revolted against God, especially in the realm of religion and morals: "they exchanged the truth of God for a lie, and worshipped and served the creature rather than the Creator" (Romans 1:25).

After this it does not surprise us when the apostle on another occasion says that the heathen are "without God" (Ephesians 2:12).

They have *religion;* nevertheless they are *without God.*

This is the Bible's description of pagan religiosity: the heathen do not come in touch with God through their religion.

This fact seems to cause us a great deal of mental difficulty.

Anyone who has any knowledge whatsoever of the checkered history of religion knows, of course, that there are heathen souls in all the pagan religions who *experience* many remarkable things. Obviously, there are heathen, too, who experience nothing, and who do not desire to experience anything. They simply drift along and do as the others do. But at the same time there are many heathen in every age who do experience strange things. They experience religious *doubt* and religious *assurance, joy* and *sorrow* in relation to the divine, repentance and *forgiveness, anxiety* and blissful *rest.*

In fact, some of the heathen mystics describe the intimate union of their souls with the divine in words which are strikingly similar to those used by Christians.

How can we account for this?

Are the experiences of the pagans all falsehood and *deception?* Of course, we meet pagans who, undoubtedly, are nothing but deceivers. But at the same time we encounter heathen whose whole life and person bear testimony to the fact that they *believe* what they say.

How is it then with these?

Are they living in a state of *self-deception?* Are their experiences purely illusory and imaginative?

Any one who would maintain this is certainly not acquainted with the remarkable history of religion. The life and work of some of these earnest and sincere pagans tell us that they are not people who live in a world of illusion and imagination.

But how can we reconcile this with the teaching of the Scriptures that the heathen, notwithstanding their religion, are without God, do not come in touch with God through their religion?

The solution to this very difficult question I do not find until I reflect upon the rich and varied world of *ideas* in which the human soul lives. We have ideas pertaining to *logic,* which are concerned with the form as well as the content of human thinking. What is *philosophy* but the unfolding of the logical ideas inherent in the human soul!

And what a rich life does not a philosopher live among these ideas!

We have *esthetic* ideas. What is art but an unfolding of the innate ideas of the human soul with regard to beauty, color, contour, rhythm, and tone? And what a rich life does not an artist live among these creations of his artistic soul!

We have *moral* ideas. What are the various moral systems but an attempt to unfold the inherent moral ideas of the human soul!

Finally we have *religious* ideas. The religions of the world are nothing else but the unfolding of the rich innate religious ideology of the soul.

That which human beings experience in all these realms is neither deception nor self-deception, but objective reality, of exceedingly great importance to human life, both in its individual and in its social aspects.

But let us keep to reality: in all these realms man experiences only and nothing else but his own ideas.

That means that in the religious realm man does not experience anything else but his own idea of God, his own consciousness of the divine. And this is precisely what the apostle said: the heathen experience religion, but not God. They are without God, notwithstanding their religion. They do not come in touch with God, but have only their own religious ideas, longings, thoughts, and feelings.

The fact that a heathen can feel either rich and happy or poor and unhappy in the practice of his religion now stands out in a new light.

As the philosopher feels poor when he is unable to unfold his innate logical ideas, and rich and happy when he is able to do so and when he can live his life among these creations of his intellect, or as the musician can suffer the worst kind of torture when his creative urge exerts itself within him without his being able to find the right tones for his motif, and, on the contrary, is most happy when he can live in the world of music which he himself has created, so will the heathen also suffer anxiety and self-reproach when his innate religious ideas exert themselves within him without his being able to live them out in his life, and, on the other hand will experience wonderful peace and satisfaction when he has succeeded in giving expression to his own religious ideas, both in his feeling, his thinking, his words, and his acts.

*With all his religion the heathen never gets beyond himself.* That is what Scripture means when it says that he is without God, notwithstanding his religion.

He experiences something, in fact, he can experience a *rich* fulness, the fulness of his own religious consciousness.

And how rich man's consciousness of the divine is, of this the history of religion tells us. Here they are arrayed side by side, all those remarkable creations which the soul of man has through the centuries spun as if by magic from his own innate religious ideology.

The fact that the Scriptures characterize all this religiosity as *sin* does not mean that the heathen should cease performing their religious rites or cease being religious. Not at all, it means that man's sin extends to his whole life, also to his religion.

Scripture shows that sin has entered into and completely permeated man's personal life, but man should not for that reason commit suicide. Sin has also entered into and permeated man's home life, but man should not for that reason cease establishing homes. Sin has entered into and permeated man's religious life, but man should not for that reason cease being religious and cease practicing religion.

On the contrary, by all this the Scriptures would tell us that man is sinful throughout, and that man must be *saved* if he is to be delivered from his personal sins, his domestic sins, his social sins, and his religious sins.

+

But here is the great danger in connection with religion. It is so easy for sinful man to look upon his religiosity, not as something which he must be saved from, but, on the contrary, as that by which he can be saved from the rest of his sins.

*Karl Barth* says somewhere that the human race has never sinned against God worse than by its religiosity.

In so doing, he does not have in mind particularly gross sins which man has at times committed in order to honor his god, such as the sacrifice of human beings, religious sexuality, or the like. What he has in mind is the attitude toward God of which this religiosity is an expression. In other things sinful man sins against himself or against some other part of creation. But in his religion he sins directly against God, robs Him of His honor, and degrades Him in a way which would be impossible outside of religion.

I am not certain that this paradox of Barth's can be defended to the last degree, though there is much in the words of the apostle, Romans 1:18 ff., which seems to indicate that Barth is in the right. But there is no doubt that Barth is right in saying that man's religiosity is actually the greatest hindrance to his being saved.

History tells us that.

We notice it first in the time of Jesus.

He encountered His greatest opposition at the hands of the *religious,* the Pharisees and the scribes. And we notice that it was their religion they made use of in opposing Him. They used it both offensively and defensively.

First they used it to shield themselves from the quiet but mighty influence which emanated from Jesus. They refused to permit themselves to be convinced of their sinfulness, either by His authoritative words, His mighty person, His miracles, which could not be successfully refuted, or by His sinless life. Then, too, they shielded themselves from Him by their punctilious fulfilment of the law, their long prayers, their frequent fastings, and their numerous alms.

They made use of their religion also to *attack* Jesus.

With gullible folk and those easily swayed in mind, they argued in the following very simple manner: We do not desire, of course, to do any harm to this religious enthusiast who is doing so much good. But we cannot quietly stand by while He seduces the chosen people of God by violating God's holy law. He exalts Himself over both the law and the temple; in fact, He even calls Himself

God. It is for religion's sake that we must eliminate Him from the populace, in order that our whole nation might not be brought under a curse because of His apostacy.

The whole *history of missions* shows us the same thing.

The greatest difficulty which the Gospel has to overcome on every mission field is the heathen religiosity of the people. It is this they use as a means of defense when the Gospel begins to convince them of sin. Personal religiosity is always the last and the most formidable defense which the Gospel must overcome on the mission fields.

This is the situation, too, in Christian lands.

In such lands there are many now who live their lives practically, if not theoretically, without religion. They feel so secure as far as God is concerned that they do not even go to the trouble of providing themselves with a religion as a shield against God.

But the yearning for eternity and the idea of God are tremendous forces, which can be suppressed for a time, it is true, but which will some day assert themselves. Religious unrest comes. Then men begin to look around for religion.

In Christian lands a person can do one of two things. *Either* become a Christian, that is, enter into fellowship with God through Christ, which means death to all selfishness and wilfulness. *Or* become *religious,* that is, turn to one's own idea of the divine, which far from putting to death our old self-life, on the contrary, gives this life of the ego religious sanction.

This decision is not an easy one to make in lands that have been Christianized, because in such countries there is general agreement that Christianity is the only real religion. These people want religion. And they want Christianity. But they would prefer to have a type of Christianity which does not hamper them in living their old self-life.

And here is where the mixing of religions comes to the assistance of modern man.

It presents a whole array of religious forms that pose as Christianity. Permit me to mention some of the best known ones: theosophy, anthroposophy, spiritism, Christian Science, and Russelism.

These I shall merely mention. Most of them are so patently different from real Christianity that anyone inquiring into the matter would be forced to recognize the difference. They are so well known and have been described so clearly and in such detail in various books and articles that I have nothing to add.

Instead, I should like to take up for discussion some modern forms of religiosity which are the more readily mistaken for real Christianity because they do not in reality constitute a system of doctrine deviating from Christianity but, on the contrary, seek as far as possible to accommodate themselves to and fit into Christian faith and doctrine.

## 1. INTELLECTUAL RELIGIOSITY

We find this as a rule among the better classes, humanly speaking. They are good, sound, well-balanced people. As a rule they come also from good Christian homes. Tact and good tone were given them as cradle-gifts.

Religion is as indispensable to them as any of the other phases of the life of the human spirit. They pray mornings and evenings. And they do not really feel right on that Sunday that they do not go to church. They partake regularly of Holy Communion. They also take part in Christian work. Not to a great extent,—they are afraid of excesses of any kind. But they are faithful and persevering in the work for which they do assume responsibility.

Their religiosity is a little dry and sober. They are, as was indicated, afraid of anything that is done to excess, and seek therefore to avoid religious enthusiasm of any kind.

Religion with them really has its stronghold in their minds, in their practical understanding of things. To them religion is an intellectual necessity. It rounds out and completes their view of life and their world-view in general. It gives an eternal perspective to their brief earthly existence, and affords them guidance and direction in their daily affairs.

They are wise, clear-headed, practical people. Their religiosity, too, is wise and practical. Simple and direct. They do not have a great deal of it, but what they do have they make use of in a sound and practical way. Oftentimes they are surprisingly bold to acknowledge that they are religious. And, practical as they are, they can often say striking things about God and religion to those with whom they associate.

They are religious, and think that they are Christians.

In their own quiet minds they no doubt think also that they are the only true Christians, who, by the grace of God, have avoided all the dangers of pietism and fanaticism.

But what strangers they are to real Christianity becomes most apparent when they on occasion come in contact with a real Christian, that is, with one to whom Christ is *life*.

They can comprehend neither the life nor the *verbal testimony* of such a person.

Such a Christian's life seems to them to be full of exaggeration and extremes. Narrow-minded and straight-laced. He neither dances nor plays cards!

Nor do they understand his speech, whether he speaks of his joys, his sorrows, or of his anxiety and distress in connection with believing the grace of God. As though anything were more simple than to believe in God! When he speaks of the cross and of the grace of God, they understand him even less than when he speaks of other things.

Yes, if he spoke Chinese to them, it would not be more incomprehensible.

They must put him in some category. Consequently they classify him either with the pietists, the fanatics, or the hysterically minded. To many these concepts are practically identical.

## 2. ESTHETIC RELIGIOSITY

We find this as a rule among people whose soul-life is rich and happy. From birth their souls have been attracted to the *unspeakable* things of life. And this is, of course, the richest phase of life.

Their finely attuned souls pick up color, form, rhythm, and melody everywhere, also in places where we ordinary, prosaically-minded folk see and hear nothing.

Moreover, their souls are never more strongly moved than when the religious chords are touched. It is in the religious realm that they really feel at home; there they feel lifted above the low and the sordid, up into the pure and the beautiful. Especially during the rendition of religious singing and other music, beneath ancient and half-lit temple-domes. Or out in God's free nature.

Nature in its grand moods means much more to them than the best sermon in a church. These are their own words. And we have no reason for doubting their sincerity.

Their life vacillates very strongly, as is the case with all emotional people. Their religiosity also is characterized by this. It may swing from the highest peaks of religious rapture and ecstasy to the lowest valleys of religious indifference and apathy.

For this reason there is little order and continuity in their religious life. Rules and regulations do not, on the whole, appeal to them. Prayer, for example, can flare up in their experience on great and emotionally rich occasions, and then be neglected again for long seasons at a time.

But this does not hinder them nevertheless from believing in their religiosity and in their relationship to God. What they experience in their great moments is to them conclusive proof that their religious affairs are in order, notwithstanding all their sins of omission and their sinful deeds. Do they not come in contact with God, and do not their little souls experience things unspeakable?

Verily, these people are religious.

They think they are Christians. Therefore they become bitter when any one tells them that their religiosity has nothing whatever in common with Christianity.

And their bitterness gives way to dumb amazement when they hear that Buddhists and other pantheists have exactly the same mystical religious experiences as they, even though the latter do not, of course, believe in Christ, yea, not even in a personal God.

A little common sense should tell them that if we really meet God in nature, then Christ is, of course, superfluous. Then the whole revelation of salvation, with God's incarnation, suffering, death, and resurrection, is all a mistake.

This is also what all religious mystics think in their innermost hearts. It is not easy for them to find any place in their thinking for Christ or for God's historical revelation on the whole. Even less for the cross and salvation. These are all redundant expressions as far as their religion is concerned, which consists merely of general religio-mystical experiences.

### 3. MORALISTIC RELIGIOSITY

Here we encounter men with strong wills, men who say: It is not enough to seek God in a bit of vague sentiment or in a brief prayer a couple of times during the

day. The important thing in religion is to *do* the will of
God, as Jesus Himself says: "For whosoever shall do
the will of God, the same is my brother."

Behold, here we have the right kind of people!

Strong, rigid idealists. Men of firm character. Men
with uncompromising wills. Strict with themselves and
with others.

In daily life they subject themselves personally to the
moral requirements of Christianity. They also strive ener-
getically, oftentimes at a great sacrifice, for a practical
carrying out of these requirements in society at large.

There is frequently something hard and uncouth about
these religious cholerics, but their fidelity to their convictions and their persistence win our respect.

Their religiosity expresses itself less in words than in
deeds. It has little of the emotional or sentimental. There
is something weather-beaten and hardy about them both
physically and spiritually.

They themselves think they are Christians.

And as a rule they think, too, that they are the only
true Christians, the only ones who make a serious business of living out the Christian religion in daily life. Moreover, they often become indignant at the sentimentality
and the effeminacy which they find in many who call
themselves Christians.

But, notwithstanding their many good sides, they are
strangers to real Christianity.

This comes to light most clearly whenever they come
in contact with Biblical preaching of conversion and regeneration. Such preaching irritates them, makes them
rebel. They look upon it as unmoral. They contend that
it dulls the human being's sense of responsibility and un-
dermines his will power. Here they encourage people to
seek a mystical experience of the divine instead of urging
them to use the little will power that still remains to them!

As previously mentioned, the greatest temptation and the greatest danger confronting a religious man has always been to look upon his *religiosity* as the means of saving himself from his sinfulness.

This becomes apparent also here. None have more difficulty accepting true Christianity than just such religious people as these.

An *ungodly* person may often be bound to his sins in an exceedingly deplorable manner, and the heart of such a person may oftentimes be tightly closed to the workings of God's grace. But regardless of the extent to which sinful lust has laid waste such a person's life, he still has this left: he knows that in matters pertaining to religion he knows nothing. It is, as a consequence, easier for him to submit to the truth of the Gospel without disputing it in any way.

The *religious* person, on the other hand, is often of the opinion that he is a specialist in things pertaining to religion. And therefore offers determined opposition to Christian preaching. At times this is done consciously; criticism is offered of Christian preaching and an attempt is made to prove that what is said is contrary both to religion and to Christianity.

This is the most common way of doing it in our day.

Years ago it was done more quietly. The spirit of self-certainty and criticism of others was not as strong as it is today. But the opposition to vital Christianity was just as great. Moreover, in those days, too, it was by means of their religiosity that men sought to shield themselves from true Christianity.

When they heard a message which urged repentance and conversion, they were strengthened in the secure feeling which they often experienced when they associated with people whose hearts were unchanged, who were worldly, ungodly, vile people.

When they heard a message pertaining to the new birth, they thanked God that they were among those fortunate ones who had been baptized in infancy.

When they heard a message which divided people into two groups: children of God and children of the world, believers and unbelievers, they felt exceedingly happy at the thought that they were one with that part of the congregation which went to church and to Holy Communion. The unbelievers,—they were those terrible people who despised all things holy and neither believed in God nor the Bible!

Within a religious armor of this kind a sinner feels quite immune to attack.

Now, as in the time of Jesus, religiosity is also used, not only as a means of *defense,* but also as a means of *attack.*

It is a painful but undeniable fact that no people are more bitterly opposed to living Christianity than these religious folk who, in their state of religious unrest, have provided themselves with an imitation of Christianity.

In fact, their bitterness is directed only against *living* Christianity. They are remarkably tolerant of all other religiosity. Indeed, even though there be but little conformity between life and teaching in such religiosity, nevertheless they are very indulgent toward it. The reason is that religiosity of this kind does not make them restless, but, on the contrary, calms them.

The reason that they are so harsh and strict in their criticism of living Christianity is that they feel constantly annoyed by it. In one way or another it speaks to their conscience and tells them that their religiosity is not Christianity, that they will be lost even though they have this religiosity, they as well as the religious Jews in the time of Jesus.

We have now briefly considered what Christianity says about religiosity and the religions of the world.

Let us now consider for a while what Christianity says about itself.

First, I would mention the fact, which no doubt stands out more clearly than anything else, that Christianity is conscious of being wholly unique.

So unique that we nowadays find it very difficult to even grasp what this means.

We are continually classifying Christianity together with the religions of the world. It is true that we do not put it on the *same* level with them; we speak of Christianity as the *highest* religion. And if we are very courageous, we speak of Christianity as the *absolute* religion. By so doing we feel that we have said the most exalted things it is possible for us to say about Christianity. And so far so good.

But the more I acquaint myself with Scriptural thinking, the clearer it becomes to me that our method of placing Christianity alongside the religions of the world is alien to the Scriptures, in fact, wholly incompatible with them.

If the religious accomplishments of the human race are sinful, if its religions put us in touch with demons and not with God, then it is clear that our way of comparing Christianity with the religions of the world is misleading, both as far as Christianity and the religions are concerned. Both are put in a false light. Christianity is drawn down, to a plane where it does not belong, yes, which is in conflict with its very nature. And the religions of the world are lifted up, to a plane where they do not belong.

If one studies the history of theology, one will find proof of this contention. Theology's attempt to find a place for Christianity among the religions, to show that Christianity is the essence and consummation of the reli-

gions of the world, has never led to anything else but
*amputation* as far as Christianity is concerned and to a
*stretching* of the religions.

Would we like to hear what Christianity has to say
about its relationship to the religions? Here it is concisely and clearly: the religions are *sin;* Christianity is
*salvation.* In the religions we are put in touch with
*demons;* in Christianity we are put in touch with *God.*

Jesus has expressed Himself about His unique position
in the following words, which I mention, not because they
are the only expressions we have, but because they are
the clearest: "No one knoweth the Son, save the Father;
neither doth any know the Father, save the Son, and he
to whomsoever the Son willeth to reveal him" (Matthew
11:27). "No one cometh unto the Father but by me"
(John 14:6).

The apostle has put it this way: "And in none other is
there salvation: for neither is there any other name under
heaven, that is given among men, wherein we must be
saved" (Acts 4:12).

+

Why does Christianity stand so entirely alone?

Why is there *salvation* nowhere else?

To this Christianity replies: "Ye worship that which
ye know not: we worship that which we know" (John
4:22). "What therefore ye worship in ignorance, this I
set forth unto you" (Acts 17:23).

Christianity says that all worship of God outside of
Christianity is idolatry. And *idolatry* consists in this, that
men worship the divine image which their own religious
consciousness has made. They neither know the living
God nor do they come in touch with Him in their religions.

In Christianity God comes down to sinful man.

The religions are nothing but man's vain attempts to lift himself up to God.

But why is it that it is only through Christianity that God will enter into fellowship with man?

Men have struggled with this question throughout all the centuries of Christianity. For it contains Christianity's mightiest stumbling-block.

To this Christianity makes reply again, concisely and clearly: God enters into fellowship with men only through Christ because He *cannot* do so in any other way.

It is our *sin* which bars the way between God and us.

The Scriptures tell us that sin is of such a serious nature, not only as far as we are concerned, but also as far as God is concerned, that He *cannot* have fellowship with sinners *without atonement*.

*Therefore* it is impossible for sinful man to lift himself up to God, though his religiosity be ever so earnest and sincere. He experiences nothing but himself, that is, the religious ideological content of his own soul.

If God was to get into touch with man and man with God, then atonement must be made for sin. And that no man was willing to do or could do, Christianity says.

God Himself had to take upon Himself the work of atonement.

This He did in Christ.

Therefore Christ is the only point where God and man can meet. And that in a most realistic sense, says Christianity. Christ is not only the only way *for us* to God; it is also the only way *for God* to us.

That is why there is salvation in none other. Therefore Christ can say: "No one cometh unto the Father but by me."

Only upon the basis of the atonement do we enter into fellowship *with God*. Up to that time we experience only our own idea of God.

And not until we enter into fellowship with God are we *saved*. For salvation is to be in touch with God. From the living God proceed the creative powers which alone can crack and break our hard, self-righteous, willful, and proud heart, yes, shatter that religiosity by means of which we individually and in groups seek to shield ourselves from the living God.

+

We have now seen *that* Christ stands alone. And *why* He stands alone among the religions.

Let us now see *how* alone He stands.

All religions stand together against Christ.

They are in other respects very different, carrying on propaganda against one another and working against one another in many ways. But on one point they stand together. They tell us, each one in its own particular way, but all as one: you must become religious, that is your only salvation; but then, too, you will be saved!

Christ stands quite alone and says: You who are evil do not become good by becoming religious. You love yourselves, and not God above all else, whether you are religious or not. And you must be *saved,* not *by* your religiosity, but *from* your religiosity, just as you must be saved from the rest of your sins.

Behold, here Christ stands alone.

All pagans, in all ages and in every land, also the pagans here in our country, think that religiosity in itself is good, that is, well pleasing to God, provided, of course, that it is not practiced dishonestly. That is why the heathen speak either of *serving* God, *worshipping* God, or *sacrificing* to God.

Christ stands entirely alone also here. He speaks of *loving* God. And He recognizes no other relationship to God but the one expressed in these words: Thou shalt *love* God above all things.

His greatest apostle says: "And if I bestow all my goods to feed the poor, and if I give my body to be burned, but have not love, it profiteth me nothing" (I Corinthians 13:3).

Here is the point at which the religious man is most certain to take offense at Christianity. As long as he thinks that salvation consists in being religious, he will calmly parry all the challenging and searching questions of the Gospel contained in these words: do you *love* God?

But from the moment that the lightning of spiritual awakening strikes down into this man's well-ordered religiosity, it will be this question which will revolutionize his whole religion. It will go like the black death through all his godliness, and lay it waste.

He begins to read the Bible. And he does so every day. Before this quieted him.

But now as he does so this painful question comes to him: "Do you love God? You have, of course, *no desire* to read the Bible; rather you feel glad every time you are through with it. You reach for the newspaper every day with keen desire and interest, but you must *compel* yourself to read the Bible each day."

He hears the Word of God. Regularly perhaps. And formerly he felt very secure as a result of his having gone to church.

But now so many annoying questions come: "Do you love God, you who feel bored as you sit in church and who wonder if the service will never come to a close, and who heave a sigh of relief when the pastor finally says, Amen, and you can get out into the open again?"

He prays to God. Perhaps every day. Formerly this made him feel secure and happy.

But now this painful question bores its way also into his prayer life: "Do you love God, you who must *force* yourself to pray a couple of minutes every day? Do you

love God, you who even during those few minutes cannot
concentrate your thoughts upon God, but find yourself
continually turning to the things which really interest you
and with which you love to occupy your mind? You cannot even recite the Lord's Prayer to its conclusion without
thinking of other things."

He fights against his sins. A little each day perhaps.
And in times past this relieved his conscience.

But now he is annoyed continually by the question:
"Do you love God, you who really have an intense desire
to sin, even though you struggle against it?"

The Scriptures describe the conversion of religious people as a *conversion from dead works.*

Now this man sees that his religiosity is nothing but
dead works, that is, works which do not spring freely and
naturally from his own inner life, but which he does,
partly from habit, partly by forcing himself more or less
to do so.

And he says to himself: God looks to the *heart.* Therefore all my pious exercises are nothing but *empty* ceremonies, because my heart is not in them. And when God
sees the sinful attitude of heart which dominates me even
during my religious exercises, He must look upon the
whole thing with abomination, as is also clearly stated in
the Scriptures: Amos 5:21; Isaiah 1:13-15.

+

Now has this man's heart been made broken and contrite.

He feels that there is nothing whole or pure in him.
Not even his religiosity, in which he formerly put full confidence. Now he sees that he must be saved from his
religiosity as he must be saved from all the rest of his sins.

As a result of the miracle of spiritual awakening he is
at last ready to become a Christian.

Now he is no longer in doubt as to the necessity of *conversion.* He sees that what he needs more than anything else is a new heart.

Now he has tested his own powers, and knows that he himself cannot change his heart. He waits for God's miracle of *regeneration.*

Now he has need of the *cross,* which always had been superfluous as far as he was concerned; it stood in the way of his former religiosity. He clings to the cross as a drowning man to a life-buoy.

It is true that he does not understand the cross. It is not possible for him to believe in the cross as he should. It is too unspeakably great for that. Can he believe that it was for him?

But in his despair and his unfeigned sincerity he now tells God the whole terrible truth.

Then the miracle takes place.

God takes this sinner up from his filth and makes him white in the blood of Christ. Permit me to use the rich and vivid figures of the Scriptures.

God opens the books of heaven and crosses out all his sins that are written there. He casts them all behind his back into the depths of the sea and remembers them no more. Then He opens the book of life and enters his name among those of all the other children of God.

Then He draws this quivering little soul to Himself, throws His eternal arms about him, and whispers into his distressed and anxious soul: "You are my child. You need have no more fears. Before you had reasons to fear, but not now. I have given Myself for your sins, and I live to help you in life, in death, and in judgment."

The bewildered little soul cannot comprehend it all at once.

He sits weeping. Now and then he sees a gleam of light, but more often he sees nothing but darkness. Nevertheless, whatever else he experiences, he clings to God in earnest prayer and confession of his sins.

Then it takes place.

The light from above falls into the darkness of his soul. Now he sees everything in the full light of God: Jesus has died for his sins. He *is* a child of God. All he needs is his Saviour!

Now it is as though his little soul would burst with jubilation.

He thanks, he praises, and magnifies the wonderful God who saves sinners.

Now the new thing has entered into his life.

He *loves* God.

That was what he lacked before. Then he was afraid when God was near. And was indifferent when God was far away.

But now he rejoices in God. Now he no longer needs to force himself to enter into the privacy of his room and pray in secret. These are now his most precious hours. He almost steals away from his fellow men in order to be alone with his God. Now he feels that he is in his element when he is with God. As a fish in water.

He is born *of* God to be *with* God. Therefore he feels that it is good to be near God.

Verily, it is the *experience* of God which is the secret of Christianity.

As long as a man only thinks about God, postulates God, longs for and reaches out after God, his relationship to God becomes only a series of onerous duties. But the moment that one *experiences* God, all this is changed.

Paul has expressed it thus: "Wherefore if any man is in Christ, he is a new creature: the old things are passed away; behold, they are become new" (II Corinthians 5:17).

God is such that all we need to do is to experience Him.

As we do so He captivates and lays hold of our hearts and binds them to Himself. We become occupied with Him instead of ourselves.

When His love becomes not only something of which we read, hear, and speak, but something which we experience, then it fills our souls.

The apostle of love breaks forth in one place and says: "Behold, what manner of love the Father hath bestowed upon us, that we should be called children of God!" (I John 3:1.)

Indeed, let us meditate upon that grace of God which saves us into *son*ship with God. He would not have us be slaves, who tremble at their master's voice and do even his slightest bidding unwillingly.

Nay, He transforms His human enemies into friends. He frees us from the spirit of bondage, and makes us children, who cry confidently, "Abba, Father!"

Christianity is, therefore, synonymous with inner freedom and joy. The Christian life is the true and the sound life.

God *woos us away* from sin.

Can you imagine anything more beautiful? With the glow of His love He melts the fetters by which we have been bound to sin. By His love He moves us to cast ourselves directly into His open arms of love. And by that same love He gives us courage to tell Him the truth, making full acknowledgment of everything to Him.

From that moment He can begin to open to us all the glory of the invisible realm. And by His love He entices us farther and farther into this invisible world.

And the more we experience in this divine realm, the easier it becomes for us to deny sin, and the more careful we become with regard to temptations of every kind.

We experience a new and rich life, which causes us to

renounce our old manner of life and to do so gladly and willingly.

Do not misunderstand me.

I do not mean that a person who has been born again is free from sin. A regenerate person also will, without doubt, experience a lack of desire for the Word of God and for prayer, and will feel unwilling to do the will of God. He will also have the painful experience of feeling a desire toward sin.

But he is acquainted also with the apostle's words of comfort to all sincere souls: "If any man sin, we have an Advocate with the Father, Jesus Christ the righteous: and he is the propitiation for our sins" (I John 2:1-2).

And not only that.

He knows that the only way to overcome sin is to experience anew the love of God in his heart. And therefore he goes directly to his Saviour and tells Him the truth, that he does not love God, but sin. And prays that He out of pure grace alone will take him to His heart again and warm his heart through and through by His wonderful love.

This is the real secret of sanctification.

This does not take place according to the will of the flesh, nor by the will of man, but by God alone. More specifically stated: It is the *experience* of God alone which can set a believer inwardly right again with respect to sin, every time the child of God because of unfaithfulness and disobedience reverts to his old way of living.